CONVERSATIONAL MAGIC

Key to Poise

Popularity and Success

Also by the Author:

How to Use Psychological Leverage to Double
the Power of What You Say, Parker,
1978.

Human Resource Development: The New
Trainer's Guide. With Edward E. Scan-
nel, Addison-Weseley, 1978.

Desk Book of New Techniques for Managing
People, Prentice-Hall, 1979.

Behavioral Supervision: Practical Ways to
Change Unsatisfactory Behavior and
Increase Productivity, Addison-Wesley,
1980.

CONVERSATIONAL MAGIC

Key to Poise,

Popularity and Success

LES DONALDSON

PRENTICE HALL
Paramus, New Jersey 07652

Library of Congress Cataloging-in-Publication Data

Donaldson, Les.
   Conversational magic.
   Includes index.
   ISBN 0-13-172155-0
   1. Conversation.   2. Success.   I. Title.
  BJ2121.D66   1981   80-26450
  158'.2   CIP

Printed in the United States of America

30 29 28 27 26 25 24

ISBN 0-13-172155-0

PRENTICE HALL
Career & Personal Development
Paramus, NJ 07652
A Simon & Schuster Company

On the World Wide Web at http://www.phdirect.com

Prentice-Hall International (UK) Limited, *London*
Prentice-Hall of Australia Pty. Limited, *Sydney*
Prentice-Hall Canada Inc., *Toronto*
Prentice-Hall Hispanoamericana, S.A., *Mexico*
Prentice-Hall of India Private Limited, *New Delhi*
Prentice-Hall of Japan, Inc., *Tokyo*
Simon & Schuster Asia Pte. Ltd., *Singapore*
Editora Prentice-Hall do Brasil, Ltda., *Rio de Janeiro*

For My Brothers

Bob and Chet

A WORD FROM THE AUTHOR

How many times have you felt, "The moment lost, the opportunity spent and now, too late, I know what to say. If only I had said . . . ." Once you read *Conversational Magic*, you can forget those feelings of distress and lost opportunity. You'll learn how to react "on the spot" without the fear of saying the wrong thing. Never again will you say to yourself, "if only I had said . . . ." From the time you read this book, you'll be saying, "I'm glad I said that," rather than, "I wish I had said . . . ."

Everyone feels an occasional "loss of words" or the inability to continue a conversation. The techniques covered in this book will help you overcome this problem. Not only will you never again experience a "loss of words," but you'll also be able to start a conversation with anyone, even a stranger, at any time and feel perfectly comfortable in doing so.

In *Conversational Magic*, the name I have chosen to express the unusually positive improvements people make in conversation with these techniques, I reveal the secrets of professional speakers and show how you can use those secrets to win the hearts and minds of all the people you meet. You will have a magic-like effect on friends and strangers alike if you practice these techniques in your daily conversation. If you want to gain pose and popularity, speed up the recognition of your abilities, and be recognized as a person on the road to success, don't stop here, read this entire book and practice all the techniques of Conversational Magic.

If you practice the techniques you learn in this book, you'll gain a psychological advantage in conversation. The myth of the "born conversationalist" is dispelled. You'll see that the basic rules of conversation are simple and easily learned. These techniques will help you gain understanding when expressing your point of view. You'll learn how to use "Conversational Magic" to increase your effectiveness and influence with other people. No matter how effective you are in dealing with people now, this book will help you become even more effective.

For example, the first three chapters of this book cover the basics of conversation. The rules followed by professional speakers, psychologists, doctors, lawyers, counselors and business managers are explained in simple terms and may be used by anyone. These techniques will help you achieve your purpose in conversation. You'll be able to tell when people are losing interest in what you say. Better still, you'll be able to develop new topics and regain the other person's interest and attention. Just from reading the first three chapters and practicing the conversational techniques explained there, you'll immediately make a more positive impression on your friends and associates, feel and act more poised, and become more popular.

Chapters 4, 5, and 6 cover methods for expanding your personality. In these chapters, I reveal secrets that have helped hundreds of people improve their conversations, gain understanding of their friends and coworkers, and become more successful. By using these successful techniques, you can add magic to your personality. You'll learn techniques to start conversations with anyone, keep the conversation interesting, and deal positively with various personality types.

In Chapters 7, 8, 9, and 10, I cover the psychological keys to improving your conversation, your understanding of other people, and your popularity. These improvement techniques will benefit you in both understanding how people think and in developing the rapport with people that is necessary for success in life in both social and business relationships.

Chapters 11, 12, and 13 are dedicated to winning commitment from other people. Chapter 11, for example, covers specific techniques for gaining support from others. You'll learn a specific five-step approach that will get people to listen to and act upon your ideas. In Chapter 12, you learn how to use psychological techniques that create obligations for other people to commit themselves to your ideas and plans. In Chapter 13, you learn the persuasion process—the key to "conversational magic."

Chapter 14 is written for the professional speaker. The techniques of developing interesting stories, developing humor, or joining any conversation without preparation, however, can be used by everyone. This chapter can give you the edge in conversation and guide you to professionalism.

Finally, in Chapter 15, I list the twelve biggest mistakes people make in conversation. This list evolved from a seven-year study of people who had experienced, as a result of their conversation, adverse consequences from their families, at work and in social situations. Each conversational mistake is clearly identified, and techniques are explained that will help you avoid making the same mistakes. By avoiding these mistakes and following the techniques explained in this book, you will improve your conversational ability and enhance your personality.

Les Donaldson

CONTENTS

1

The Psychology of Conversational Magic

In this chapter we will show you how you can put "magic" into your conversation. You'll discover that there are many good speaking styles that contain elements of conversational magic. You'll find you can use the guidelines in this chapter to build the magic you need to give you poise, popularity, and success.

Consider the psychological factors that influence people in coversation. For example, you may make a sarcastic remark that will irritate the person to whom you are speaking. That irritated person, having had his defense mechanism triggered, may respond in anger. This in turn may anger you. Soon a full-blown argument is in progress, and it somehow must be "cooled" if you are to resume friendly conversation.

Psychological factors such as anger and defensiveness become *barriers* to good conversation. You'll learn how to recognize psychological barriers, how to neutralize them with techniques of conversational magic, and how to begin to develop the expertise that will enhance your poise, improve your conversational personality, and build your success as a conversationlist.

The techniques described in this book are based on my own personal study of the responses of people in conversation. I have done research on how people react to various techniques in conversation, and I will show you how to apply these techniques.

The psychology of conversation includes the philosophy of human acceptance. Everybody tries to gain acceptance by others. Through our conversations we all attempt to gain acceptance, respect, friendship, safety, and growth. The magic in conversation lies in using talk between people to satisfy their psychological needs. Conversation, then, is a key tool in fulfilling human needs.

PSYCHOLOGICAL TECHNIQUES THAT ADD INTEREST TO YOUR CONVERSATION

There are three psychological techniques that form the basis for conversational magic. These three basic techniques are so powerful in gaining respect, understanding, and interest that they alone will provide a pathway to poise, popularity and success. You can employ them immediately in your daily conversations with your friends and acquaintances. This practice will ensure your eventual mastery of conversational magic.

The First Rule of Successful Conversation

The first technique is to listen to the other people who are engaged in conversation. By listening carefully to others, you learn the things that interest them. Then you can relate to those areas of interest and this will increase your popularity. Everyone likes a person who responds to his area of interest.

Of course, the more you listen, the more you learn about others. Listening requires you to be silent; you can't listen and talk at the same time. Carlyle said, "Silence is more eloquent than words." An old Latin proverb gives a clue to the value of silence. "Keep quiet and people will think you a philosopher." Silence should not be overdone, however, as real listening requires proof. After the person speaking pauses, ask a question or give your feelings or opinion of what was said. Obviously you cannot make comments or ask questions unless you were listening. Those comments and questions are the proof that you were listening and the assurance that you will gain popularity.

The Second Rule of Successful Conversation

The second psychological technique, asking questions, relates closely to the first in that questions show interest and respect. When you ask a question it proves your interest. When you ask a question that requires the other person to give an opinion or make an evaluation, you are showing that you respect the other person's opinion. If you did not respect it, you would not ask for it.

Obviously, your questions must be sincere. Ask questions about topics the other person has some knowledge of. If you attempt to fool your companion by pretending respect when none exists, he will see through this and you will lose rather than gain popularity.

The best way to ensure sincerity in your questioning is to ask questions that will give you some information to increase your knowledge. An old English proverb points out the fallacy of insincere questions. It goes, "A fool may ask more questions in an hour than a wise man can ask in a year."

Some people feel asking questions is an imposition on the other person. This just isn't true. The truth is, questioning shows respect and is the only way to really understand the other person. Ted Harley, a friend from Texas, tells a story that exemplifies this fallacy. "A doctor was questioning a stubborn Texas farmer. The farmer snorted that he wasn't going to answer a lot of questions, it was up to the doctor to find out what was wrong. The doctor replied that the farmer would have to call in a veterinarian. Only a veterinarian could make a diagnosis without asking questions."

The Third Rule of Successful Conversation

The third technique for successful conversation is to talk about the other person's goals and plans. People are motivated to talk about their own goals and plans by the same emotional energy that provides the drive to reach their goals and realize their plans. You can become a more successful conversationalist simply by asking people to tell you their plans for the future or their goals for the following year.

Many people have problems in conversation because they use too much energy trying to think of something to say. If you have this problem, correct it by turning your attention to the other person. Concentrate on getting him to talk about his plans or goals for the future. You might always be prepared with a few questions to get him started talking, then your own thoughts will be triggered naturally by what he reveals to you.

Once the person reveals one plan, you can ask further questions about that plan. For example, if someone says he plans to find a new job next year, you can ask, why, where, how and what kind. All sorts of comments and questions about work and job hunting will naturally evolve from these questions.

Everyone has times when he simply doesn't feel like talking. If you are questioning someone who just doesn't respond, don't make a big deal out of it. Ask a question about his feelings or opinions and then comment on your own feelings or opinions that relate to the same topic.

It's never a good idea to ask people why they are not talking or why they don't have much to say. This may embarrass them and encourage them to avoid you in the future. I have an acquaintance who seldom talks much, but attends a number of business meetings. Because he is often reminded that he hadn't said anything, he has developed a standard remark to defend himself. He replies, "You were talking so fast, it took all my energy to listen." He might reply, "Your topic was so interesting, I was concentrating on listening," if he chose to be polite.

Another friend, who is known for his humorous remarks, once was asked if he didn't have anything to add to the conversation. He replied, "I had one thought, but it was so lonely, it went away." The better technique is to ask your acquaintance to comment on his plans or goals rather than confront him about his lack of conversation.

Edna Scott's Coffee Break Magic

I recently noticed that one of the Marketing Associates in our office, Edna Scott, used her coffee break to take a short nap. I wondered if she were really this tired, or if she had some problem. I began to watch her each day and soon became sure that her workload was not overly heavy; there must be some problem bothering her. I noticed that she rarely talked to anyone, so I decided to talk to her and see if I could help.

To my surprise, she eagerly responded to my questions and comments. She was very interesting and full of enthusiasm. We talked for quite awhile, and during the conversation she revealed her plans to leave the company. She said that I was the only one who had talked to her in weeks.

Edna's planned resignation was three weeks away, so I asked her if she would be willing to test the three rules of successful conversation for me before she left. The idea intrigued her and I gave her a card listing the three rules.

1. Listen for things that interest other people and relate to those interests in your conversation.
2. Ask questions to show interest and respect.
3. Talk about the other person's goals and plans.

Edna took the test to heart. She quickly memorized the three rules and began to use them immediately. Edna moved out, on her coffee break, and began to talk to people. Slowly more and more people began to seek her out. Edna developed the conversational magic that attracted people to her. By showing interest in their problems, plans, and goals and by showing respect for their ideas and opinions, she became the most popular member of the group.

I noticed that Edna did not leave the company. The psychological techniques that she utilized to develop conversational magic gave her a new interest and a reason to stay with the company.

HOW PSYCHOLOGY CAN HELP YOU ACHIEVE YOUR PURPOSE IN CONVERSATION

You can use tested psychological techniques to achieve your purpose in conversation. Often people feel frustrated because they can't get people to listen to their ideas or opinions and consequently can't achieve their purpose in conversation. Five simple steps based on psychological principles will help you achieve your purpose in conversation even under adverse circumstances. They are:

1. Clear Away the Storm Clouds
2. Project a Benefit
3. Blend Ideas
4. Check Commitment
5. Give Assurance

Clear Away the Storm Clouds

Often some obstruction or barrier interferes in conversation and keeps your message out. For example, if a person is excited about something, especially a personal achievement, all of his or her attention will be directed to that event. That person will not listen, in fact, cannot listen, until the internal energy that directs his or her interest and creates the excitement subsides. To you, that excitement may be a storm cloud blocking out your message, but to the other person it is the most important thing in the world.

To clear away the storm clouds, you must help the other person expend the emotional energy that supports that excitement. You do this, you clear away the storm clouds, by encouraging the excited or distracted person to talk it out. As one talks, he experiences excitement and releases energy. He finally exhausts his own excitement and is then psychologically ready to listen to you.

You can help the other person expend this emotional energy by listening attentively, by asking for detailed information and by making complimentary remarks. You will then be appreciated by the other person. He or she will recognize the fact that you listened and will feel obligated to listen to you.

Project a Benefit

Once you have cleared away any distracting interference, you then must develop the other person's interest in your topic. One way to do that is to project a benefit. Point out some benefit he can derive from your idea or point of view. Show how the person's health, wealth or happiness will be improved. People listen to ideas they benefit from.

My friend Tim Harley, the self-proclaimed "hottest humorist from Houston," once said he could immediately get anyone's attention by relating to survival. He demonstrated his techniques for me by taking me along on a sales call. He explained that the account he was calling on was a very difficult one. The buyer, according to Tim, was so mean and miserable that two different salesmen had tried to run him down in their cars last Christmas.

It was just before Thanksgiving when we made the call. True to Tim's description, the buyer seemed to be very difficult. "Well what are you doing here," snapped the buyer. Tim replied with his guaranteed attention getter. "I have an idea that will make sure you're one turkey that gets safely through Thanksgiving."

Blend Ideas

A method for getting your ideas accepted is to blend your ideas into some of the other person's words, phrases, or ideas. If you can use some of the more preferred words and phrases of the other person, he or she will be flattered by the use of his own words and more receptive to your ideas.

I have a friend, for example, who consistently uses the phrase "systematic investigation." If I want this friend to listen, all I have to do is to talk about a "systematic investigation" of the current topic and he is all ears.

The blending of ideas is an even more effective method of persuasion. If you can blend your ideas into one previously expressed by the person you are trying to persuade, your acquaintance will be more likely to accept it. After all, he or she already believes part of it. It's simply a matter of seeing how the two fit together.

Will Hastings, an Arizona business executive, is very effective in blending ideas as a method of persuasion. Will is an excellent conversationalist, who realizes that persuasion occurs only when the conversation is understood and related to, in a personal way, by the other person. Will was talking to an Arizona legislator recently and demonstrated the blending technique for my benefit.

The legislator was well known for his liberal policies. He is a dedicated public servant and truly concerned for the welfare of our citizens. Will understood the legislator's concern for the poor but believed his methods inflationary and actually harmful to the poor in the long run. Will's intention was to blend his anti-inflation message into one of the legislator's pet sayings, "All our material wealth is useless unless it benefits the poor as well as the rich."

Will began by saying to the legislator, "Bob, I know of your great concern for the poor, and I would like to discuss a few ideas that I believe will help you become more successful in your attempts to raise their standards of living. I think inflation hurts the poor far more than it hurts those earning more than an average wage.

"For example, I have a friend who made $75.00 a week in 1973. By 1976 his wages had increased to $90.00 a week. Now, statistically he had kept up with the rate of inflation. The problem is that the basic necessities of life had gone up at 4 to 5 times the general rate of inflation. The overall inflation rate had been averaged out to a considerably lower figure than the rise in basic necessities."

Will asked for and got the legislator's promise to fund his social programs with tax revenues and not from inflationary techniques. *The blending of the idea that inflation is an "invisible tax" that falls more heavily on the poor with the legislator's idea that the poor in our country should share in our material wealth* formed an irrefutable argument.

Check Commitment

The fourth step in achieving your purpose in conversation is to check for commitment. Often we are so certain of our own ideas or of our ability to persuade others that we assume the other person agrees with what we have said. Often, this is not true. Many people are too polite to mention the fact that they do not share our opinion.

Just because one responds with, "Yes," "Uh huh," and "I see" doesn't mean he agrees with what is being said. It simply means that he is listening, hears, understands, or that he recognizes that you are talking.

To find out if you are achieving your purpose, you must ask. You might say, "Do you agree?", or better still, "How do you feel about this?", or "How would you use this idea?" Any question that requires the other person to commit to the idea or commit to the use of the idea tells you whether or not you are achieving your purpose.

Give Assurance

The final step, after some action has been taken or some statement of commitment has been made by the other person, is to give some assurance that he or she has made the right decision. Everyone feels some discomfort after changing a position or making a decision that is not completely consistent with previously held beliefs.

One way that we convince ourselves that we have made the correct decision is through the feedback—the assurances—that we get from others. Any comment such as, "You've made the right decision," "Your acceptance of this idea will help you," or simply "You're doing the right thing," will assure him and help you achieve your purpose in conversation.

How Carey Smith Used Conversational Magic and Became an Interesting Conversationalist

Carey Smith was a "conversational iceberg." When she met someone new, went to a party or met an acquaintance on the street, she completely froze. Carey's inability to enter friendly conversations with people developed into a fear that kept her from going to parties, accepting social engagements, or appearing in any public place where she would be likely to be involved in conversation.

Carey may have carried this burden for many years, except for a chance remark that she overheard when passing my office. I had remarked to a friend that I could teach "conversational magic" to anyone who could memorize four words. Carey came back after my friend left and asked about "conversational magic." She wanted to know specifically if memorizing four words would help her overcome her fear of speaking.

I pointed out the four words were merely "trigger" words that would help her develop the self-confidence necessary to overcome the psychological blocks that kept her from becoming an interesting conversationalist. I wrote the four words out for her on a card, as follows:

1. *Listen*, (without interrupting the other person).
2. *Question* (for background information on the person or the topic).

3. *Encourage* (idea expansion).
4. *Discuss* (the other person's plans and goals).

After a brief discussion of the psychological importance of the four words, I asked her to try the system for a week and then let me know how it worked.

After the first week-end, Carey was back in my office, all smiles telling me how well the system worked. She had a wonderful time talking to many people, and one girl had invited her to a party the following Saturday night. For the first time, she looked forward to going out.

OVERCOMING PSYCHOLOGICAL BARRIERS THAT BLOCK YOUR CONVERSATIONAL POTENTIAL

Psychological barriers that block the realization of your potential may be grouped into two major classifications, (1) those that are behavioral in nature and interfere with your natural desire to attain popularity or cause you to lose some measure of the popularity you already have and (2) those self-restraining barriers that keep you from growing into a more mature, a more engaging, a more exciting and entertaining personality. As we discuss these two classifications of psychological barriers, note the barriers that may be holding you back so that you can work on their elimination with techniques explained in this book.

Barriers That Cause a Loss of Popularity

Friendship has been described as "a level of understanding that protects the friend's feelings against sarcasm, anger, ignorance and most other human errors." Popularity, however, does not automatically result from friendliness. Popularity depends upon your understanding other people and making sure you do nothing to offend them, even in jest. There are numerous behavioral barriers that block the attainment of, or cause the loss of, popularity. We'll look at the three most common as examples of the type behavior you should avoid in conversation in order to increase your popularity.

The misguided Arrow. I have a friend, Tommy Arrow, who is a highly educated college professor. Tom, a real intellectual who is loaded with interesting stories of his childhood on an Indian Reservation, could be a very popular person. Tom's popularity, however, is very low. Tom attracts attention and interest with his childhood stories, and as his popularity begins to build he eventually "pops off" with what I call his misguided arrows—sarcasm.

Tom knows his misguided arrows have cost him the richly deserved popularity he would otherwise have. We have discussed the problem from time to time as his popularity rises and falls, trying to find a reason for the sarcasm and a way to stop it. Tom has not been able to stop it alone, as it is not intentional. He makes sarcastic remarks spontaneously without intending to hurt anyone or even realizing why he does it.

Tom recently was passed for a promotion that he was well qualified for. We decided that Tom's sarcasm had cost him the job. At that point, I recorded the remarks Tom made and jotted down notes describing the circumstances. At first I could find no pattern. Tom slung his arrows in all situations with all kinds of people. It seemed to make no difference to him whether we were talking to students, faculty, businessmen, or other social groups, it was always the same. At some point in the conversation, as if compelled by some mystical power, Tom would make a sarcastic remark.

Being unable to find anything in the social situation (after poring over a years' notes) that triggered Tom's sarcasm, I turned my attention to the nature of the sarcasm. The remarks were loaded with subtle humor. They were paraphrases, analogies and anecdotes that were full of intellectual wit and humor. "At last," I thought, "I've found the answer. Tom is trying to be funny."

In discussing my findings with Tom, it soon became obvious that I had erred in my assumption. Tom convinced me that he was not trying to be funny. His sarcasm, he felt, was an automatic response to something other people said, rather than a conscious effort on his part to get people to laugh. Since Tom was generally considered a serious type, I bought his argument and began my search again.

I had almost given up, when one day, Tom and I attended a professional meeting together and were seated at a table with an extremely arrogant colleague. This arrogant man slowly put down all those at the table by criticizing their reason, their opinions and their evidence.

Inevitably he crossed words with Tom. With one stinging sarcastic remark, Tom demolished the man. Tom's remark clearly established him as intellectually superior to the arrogant protaganist who quickly began to talk with someone else. Tom, without thinking, turned and said to me, "That little pearl of wisdom was worthy of Will Bender himself." I questioned Tom about Will, as I had never heard him mentioned before.

Will, it turns out, was the leader of a group of verbal combatants that Tom belonged to in college. Membership in the group depended upon the members being able to think up intellectual "barbs" or remarks with double meanings. The more intellectually subtle, the higher the prestige of the group. Will, of course, had established himself as the group leader by the use of his intellectual capacity to develop these subtle remarks.

It was all clear now. In the discussion that followed, Tom clearly saw his reason for using sarcasm. The sarcasm came out during intellectual discussion. Tom was subconsciously using it to prove his intellectual ability. He was still competing with Will to retain his place in the group. Once fully aware of his motivation, Tom was able to stop. As he eliminated his use of sarcasm, his popularity began to increase. Today, five years later, he is one of the most popular people on campus.

The sideswipe. The most serious of all barriers is the sideswipe. When you sideswipe someone you push him off the track, stop him, block him out, deny him the right to finish expressing his thought, opinion or statement. As you've probably guessed, a sideswipe is an interruption. When you interrupt the person who is speaking to you, you set up a psychological barrier so great that it can lead to frustration, anger, and argument. At the very least, it creates an impression of you as an inconsiderate egotist and causes a loss of your popularity.

Blocking the expression of an opinion, as interrupting does, frustrates the psychological drives that originally motivated the person to express himself. The interruption, then, blocks the psychological energy that is normally released with the expression of the opinion. The frustration, now driven by the sideswiped energy, will be turned against you in anger. Some people will express this anger verbally, by pointing out that you have interrupted or by asking you to wait until they have finished. But many will say nothing; they turn the energy inward to build an "unpopular image" of you.

You can avoid sideswiping your friends' ideas by listening carefully to make sure they've finished before you speak. If you're not sure, ask, "Are you finished?" If you catch yourself involved in a "sideswipe," pull over, stop, and apologize.

The sunshine shot. The third most serious barrier to increasing popularity is ignoring people. If you know someone who never stops to listen to your ideas, never gives you the time to express an opinion, or is too busy to say, "Good morning," you'll probably find that person is always available to receive a little praise. As a matter of fact these types of people always seem to have time only for self-praise—what I call the "sunshine shot." Things are only sunny when pointed their way.

I have a friend in San Francisco, Hank, who has a knack for describing situations such as this. Hank says, "A person who won't take the time to say good morning isn't worth the time it takes to mourn their passing by."

No one likes to be ignored, and when it happens, we feel hurt or frustrated and develop a dislike for the person who ignored us. This creates a barrier to the popularity of one who ignores people. Everyone who wishes to gain popularity would be well advised to be courteous enough to give *special attention* to everyone they meet and converse with. Emerson said, "Life is not so short but that there is always time enough for courtesy." To make sure this barrier is not blocking your attempts to gain popularity, spend a little extra time paying special attention to the friends you meet tomorrow.

You can pay special attention by asking about something that you know your friend is interested in. Then pay close attention to what your friend says. Make some comment or ask some further question related to a point your friend made. This is the beginning of conversational magic, the proof that you are truly interested and are paying special attention to your friend's comments.

One of the most popular people I know, Frank Garland, always pays special attention to whomever he is conversing with. Frank is a natural conversationalist, bubbling with enthusiasm, with a thousand stories to tell, and with the magic excitement that comes from a love of friendly conversation. Frank holds everyone's attention. Yet, Frank is always aware of the other person, he has the time and shows courtesy to the other person. He shows special attention to anyone who wishes to speak, and, in so doing, enhances his own popularity.

Barriers That Block Personality Growth

There are certain psychological barriers that keep us from reaching the full potential of our personality. We may wish to be outspoken and friendly, yet something holds us back. We may feel an urge to tell a story to a group or strike up a conversation with a friend, yet we fear the consequences. We feel we may be ineffective, become embarrassed, or be ridiculed. These fears are psychological barriers that impede our personality growth.

These fear-related barriers can be overcome. By simple trial and evaluation you can remove barriers. By taking one small step at a time, carefully evaluating the results of each step, and making corrections where necessary, you can eliminate these barriers one by one.

A number of cases of people who were actually afraid to leave their own homes have recently come to light. Their fear of meeting people kept them bound inside their homes, devoid of the pleasure of human companionship. Psychologists have led many of these people through a step-by-step process of personality growth that moved them first just out of the door and back. Then up the block and back. Then to a shopping center and back. And finally, these people have been able to actually go inside a department store, shop and mingle with people. By comparison, the barriers that keep most of us shy and reticent are minor irritations that with a little effort can be easily overcome.

Mary Wilson, a shy high school graduate, overcame these barriers when she realized they were controlling her life and blocking her personality growth. She found it extremely difficult to talk to people, even though she felt lonely and frustrated. Mary, determined to overcome her problem, talked her employer into giving her a chance as a receptionist.

Being a receptionist was very difficult for Mary. Twice she decided the pressure of talking to strangers was too great to bear. Twice she decided to quit, but each time her determination brought her through the ordeal. Slowly, Mary began to feel more comfortable in conversation. Little by little she developed the confidence to talk to anyone. Mary's popularity increased as her new-found confidence spilled over and helped her develop the conversational magic that gained her the popularity she had previously been denied. Today Mary is both popular and happy because she overcame the barriers that had blocked her personality growth.

The Psychological "Cooling System"

The psychological "cooling system" is a technique of conversational magic that is sure to increase your popularity. The psychological cooling system removes the emotional barriers that block understanding and create unfriendly feelings.

When you encounter someone who is angry, scared, excited, bewildered or in any way emotionally excited, you can use the psychological "cooling system" to help him release the pent-up emotional energy that accompanies any emotional turbulance. You simply deal with the emotion and ignore the content of the message.

Your natural inclination at this point will be to help solve the problem, offer consolation, or in some cases be critical, defensive or promise to correct those things that are under your control. All of these things are wrong because they do not permit the release of the emotional energy that supports the anger, excitement, etc.

The problem of suppressing this emotional energy is that it forces expression in some other form. If the emotional energy can't be talked out, it may be released in the form of anger or accident. The teenager who comes home from school excited about some scholarly achievement needs an opportunity to talk out the underlying emotional energy—to express the excitement. If the parent cuts the teenager off by demanding some immediate chore or by criticizing some previous rule infraction, the teen-ager's emotional energy will be expressed in some other way.

In one case, a teen-ager was interrupted and told to wash the dishes left from the morning breakfast before saying a word. This youngster unintentionally broke two dishes and a cup, before breaking down and crying. Obviously, lack of parental courtesy was clearly to blame. The system devised by Dr. Carl Rogers to deal with emotionally distressed patients, which I call the psychological "cooling system," can be used to resolve these problems.

The psychological "cooling system" deals with the problem of releasing the energy by permitting the emotionally excited person to continue talking until the emotional energy is talked out. You do this by repeating the emotional statement made by the other person. In the case of the teen-ager who comes in with a shout, "Hey I got an "A." you would respond, "Oh, you got an 'A'?" After the teen-ager replies then ask him to tell you all about it. In other words, ask some question that gives the youngster an opportunity to express the rest of the emotional energy.

The same technique is effective in dealing with anger. One who argues with an angry person makes an enemy. One who helps an angry person by listening while he talks out the emotional energy wins friendship and popularity. When you en-counter someone who says, "I'm mad," simply repeat their statement. Say, "You're mad?" or "I see you're mad," and wait for them to say it all. After he has expressed the anger, he will usually be willing to discuss the problem rationally.

By using the psychological "cooling system," you will win friends and eliminate the barriers that interfere with your at-tempts to increase your popularity. As you practice this technique, it may seem uncomfortable at first, but as you see the positive results of your rise in popularity, you will feel complete-ly comfortable.

Bob Moreland's Successful First Attempt at Using the Psychological "Cooling System"

Bob Moreland is the evening division coordinator for a west coast community college. Recently, a distraught transfer stu-dent came into Bob's office, obviously excited. "I have been told that I can only transfer 6 units to this school. I earned 18 units in an out-of-state school and I'm only permitted to transfer 6 units," raged the student. "What's wrong with you people anyway?"

Bob, having recently been trained in the use of the psychological cooling system, realized this student needed time to expend the pent up emotional energy. "I see that you're upset," remarked Bob.

"You bet your 'fanny' I'm upset," retorted the student. "You people are insensitive to the problems of your students."

Bob used the "mirror" technique, "You feel we are insensitive?"

"You bet I do," replied the student. "I feel like I've wasted a years' work. Now I'm going to have to take the same courses over again. No one likes to do the same work twice."

Notice that the student began to explain how the policy was affecting him. This explanation of the problems that he felt is an indication that the emotional energy has subsided. At this point Bob was able to deal with the student on a rational basis. By concentrating on the problems, Bob was able to help the student work out a class schedule that permitted him to finish the educational requirements without repeating courses and in the minimum possible time.

Bob later said he felt satisfied that he had done a much better counselling job than he had in the past, simply by using the psychological cooling system.

2

Determining How Your Conversational Impact on People Affects Your Popularity

The desire for acceptance and friendship in our society has resulted in a conversational preference for polite compliments and a bias against constructive criticism. Even though it is accepted by society that polite criticism is a healthy food for a growing personality, individual members of our society cling to the security of polite conversation and refuse to give us the negative feedback or constructive criticism that we need to improve our popularity. To become more popular, however, we need this constructive feedback. It's our only means of seeing ourselves as others see us.

In this chapter, you'll see how to overcome this problem. There are four non-threatening ways to determine how much impact your conversation has on people. By learning these techniques and the conversational clues that reveal how people feel about you, you'll be able to root out people's negative thoughts and improve your impact on others. The examples covered in this chapter will also help you develop the conversational magic that will improve your impact on people and increase your popularity.

FOUR WAYS TO DETERMINE HOW MUCH IMPACT YOUR CONVERSATION HAS ON PEOPLE

People unintentionally let us know how much impact we have, in spite of their unnecessarily polite intentions. They inform us how interesting we are, how important what we say is to them, and how committed they are to what we ask of them or to the ideas we express. Without being aware of the message they send, they communicate in their conversation and in their actions the answer to how much impact we have. The four following techniques will help you find how much impact you have on people in conversation.

Listen For Irrelevancy

One way to determine whether or not you're making an impression on the person you're speaking to is to listen for irrelevant remarks. If he keeps saying things that do not relate to the subject you are trying to discuss, those irrelevant observations tell you that your comments are not having any impact. The other person does not care for the things you are saying.

Because what you say is not interesting to the other person does not mean there is anything wrong with what you are saying. It simply means the other person is not interested in that particular topic at that particular time, for some one of any number of reasons.

The most usual reason for this lack of attention is the other person's preoccupation with some unfinished activity. This may be either a physical or a mental activity. Human nature is such that once we decide upon an activity, whether it be finishing a task or expressing an idea, we are motivated to complete it. If the completion of that activity is interfered with by some obstacle, such as conversation about a different subject, the psychological energy keeps driving the activity back into operation. This energy is often expressed as an irrelevant remark.

Any remark that relates to something other than the topic you are discussing is an irrelevant remark. It is always a clue that the other person has something more pressing on his mind than the topic you are trying to discuss. You can improve your impact on people by listening for irrelevancy and exploring its meaning. By dropping your own topic and concentrating on the topic introduced in the irrelevant remark, you help the other person complete the unfinished activity. This completion will remove the psychological energy that had built up. Since a person feels good after finishing something, he will feel good toward you for helping him talk the problem through.

Sometimes, however, a partner in conversation never stops talking. Some people introduce one irrelevancy after another and never let *you* talk. There are different reasons for this impolite conversational behavior. Some people simply feel they have to keep the conversation going and think that if they stop for a moment they will have to face what to them is a dreadful silence. Other people think that only *their* thoughts and ideas are important. No matter what the reason, once this talkative behavior becomes a habit, it is very difficult to deal with. One way is to steadfastly keep bringing the conversation back to the point you wish to complete by saying, "Excuse me, I would like to finish this point." Don't expect too much from this type of person. No matter how long you listen, your companion never finishes. Mark Twain usually handled these situations with humor.

One story about Mark Twain (Samuel Clemens) illustrates his technique. He was the guest of honor at a New York opera box-party. The hostess had irritated him by her constant chatter. Mr. Clemens had controlled his anger throughout the performance but could not refrain from a parting humorous shot. When the evening had drawn to a close, the hostess added the crowning blow that gave him his opportunity for revenge.

"Mr. Clemens," the hostess fawned, "I do hope you will join us next week again, when the opera will be *Tosca*. I'm sure you'll like it." "I'd be delighted," exclaimed Mr. Clemens, "I've never heard *you* in that." Although effective for him, this cutting or sarcastic type humor would usually not be effective for those of us who are not as popular as Mr. Clemens.

Watch For Non-Verbal Clues

Many people err in offering free advice. If you start giving people unsolicited advice, your popularity will drop in a hurry. If you don't believe this, just ask a few people. The next time you see a friend, say, "Hi, Mary, would you like some advice?" After asking a few people, you'll get the picture. Only about one person in 100 in our society wants advice. This reluctance to accept advice is changing to a small degree as people are introduced to non-threatening ways to receive advice and criticism. Many people have learned to accept advice and criticism from "encounter" groups, self-help clubs such as Toastmasters, or other social groups.

People also give non-verbal clues that will tell you the kind of impact you are having on them. If you offer advice, for example, and they don't like it, they will flinch, frown, twiddle their fingers, look away or shuffle their feet, etc. All of these nervous or "cool" reactions are clues that you are having a negative impact. If, on the other hand, your companion reacts warmly, smiles, acts open and enthusiastic, you can be sure that you are having a positive impact on him.

Let's suppose you are talking to a close friend, and you start explaining the plans you have made for the two of you for the day. You notice that your friend's brow begins to tighten, a frown forms, and the friend seems somewhat less than enthusiastic. Obviously, these non-verbal clues show that your friend doesn't like your plans. Your impact is negative. Anyone would recognize those clues, right? No! Not necessarily.

Often we become so enthusiastic about our own plans or ideas that we close our minds to others. We fail to notice the feedback that we get from people. The frown or nervous shuffling escapes our attention because, in our overly enthusiastic state, we direct our attention inwardly to our own interests.

You can overcome this problem. By developing the habit of always watching for non-verbal clues, you will automatically still notice them when you become excited or enthusiastic. Simply because you begin to observe these clues your impact on people will be strengthened. You will unconsciously correct any negative behavior in response to the non-verbal feedback; this will result in a more positive impact. Of course your conscious awareness of non-verbal clues will also help you consciously correct those actions that irritate and affect other people negatively.

Indications of Interest

I have a sign that says, "NO HELP WANTED—I make enough mistakes on my own." Whether it's offering help, giving advice, or just plain talking, we can't assume the other person is interested. Just as there are non-verbal signs that indicate the level of interest, there are also verbal indications.

If someone asks you a question about the topic you are discussing, that is a clear indication of interest. Only a person who was interested enough to have listened to what you previously said could ask the question. Generally, people are not going to ask a question unless they are interested in the answer.

Another indication of interest is a closely related comment or opinion. If the person to whom you are speaking makes a comment about the topic, that is an indication of interest. If the comment relates to some personal aspect of the other person's life, the interest is higher. Either questions or closely related comments are indications that you are having a positive impact on the other person.

One word of caution, don't assume that everyone who doesn't show verbal indications of interest isn't listening. There is always a poker face around who doesn't show any emotion, no matter how interesting the topic. One woman who thought her husband never listened, found that he heard everything that was important to him.

One night this woman pulled her drunken husband out of a bar and was leading him home when a storm came up unexpectedly. The wind blew the power lines down, and in the dark the couple fell in a ravine that was rapidly filling with water. The frightened lady, clutching her husband's hand, whispered quietly, "Lord, please get me and my drunken husband safely out of this ravine." The husband quickly remarked, "Tell him I'm sick, don't say I'm drunk."

Clues to Commitment

The highest level of impact that you can ever achieve is to have someone become committed to an idea or action as a result of your verbal persuasion. This doesn't happen too often, and when it does, you can be very proud.

The verbal clues to commitment are not simple statements that the other person agrees with you, but rather statements of action. The plans, details, and time schedules of how he intends to use your idea show commitment.

If he is not really committed to your idea, you will be able to tell because he will not be able to give you a plan of action or any details of putting the plan into action.

CONVERSATIONAL CLUES THAT REVEAL
HOW PEOPLE FEEL ABOUT YOU

Often we come to erroneous conclusions about other people's feelings about us. We may think people care for us who don't, or conversely we may think people don't like us when they actually do. These conclusions can result in misguided actions or unnecessary loneliness.

There are three simple techniques that you can use to determine how people feel about you. These are checking compliments for sincerity, recognizing phrases that reveal negative feelings, and recognizing phrases that reveal positive feelings.

Checking Compliments for Sincerity

Although politeness and courtesy are admirable traits, they are often overdone. People act unduly polite and pay compliments that are undeserved. Unfortunately, most of us are easily deceived by unwarranted compliments and flattery. Although this insincerity is rampant in our culture, it is not new. Homer spoke of it in the *Iliad*.

> Hateful to me as are the gates
>   of hell,
> Is he, who hiding one thing
>   in his heart,
> Utters another.

Sincere compliments can be recognized because they contain a reference to some specific item or act that deserves the compliment. For example, "You really look sharp today," may or may not be sincere. However, "You really look sharp in that brown suit," is more likely to be sincere because it ties in to a specific item, the brown suit. Of course a compliment related to a specific accomplishment is also usually sincere.

Insincere flatterers often give themselves away. My friend Frank Garland, who was known to bestow a "bit of the old blarney" on occasion, tells how he was caught in the act of complimenting without proper cause.

Frank had become carried away and told a quite homely young lady, "Nothing could be more beautiful than you." She, embarrassed and well aware of her homeliness, was determined to embarrass Frank in order to teach him to be less deceitful when talking to people.

The young lady approached Frank shortly thereafter and introduced her sister who was truly beautiful. "You described me as though nothing could be more beautiful," said the young lady. "What do you think of my sister?"

Frank, for a moment visibly shaken at his own and the sister's embarrassment, recovered his composure and replied, "Forgive me if I was a bit too enthusiastic. But, I did not dream that I would have an occasion to compare mortals such as you and I with one so heavenly."

Phrases That Reveal Negative Feelings

People often reveal negative feelings by building subtle sarcasm, mild criticism or derisive humor into their conversation. When you find this sarcasm, criticism, and derision being continually directed at you, you can be sure it's not just a joke. Whether admitted or not, these belittling phrases are being used to express negative feelings about you. This obviously means that something about you has offended the other person. The best corrective action is simply to ask if you have done or said something to offend him. Usually he will tell you, and then you can decide how to correct the situation.

Should the other person say that you have not offended him, then tell him that he has unintentionally offended you. Point out that although you are sure he means no offense, the constant sarcasm, criticism, and derision is very offensive. This should end the problem. If not, stop associating with the offensive person.

The best example of sarcasm that I've heard is when a husband noticed his wife packing away her winter clothes. He reminded her to pack the clothes carefully or the moths would get to them. "You don't have to worry about moths getting to my plush imitations; they'll spend their time getting at the genuine seal-skin owned by the lady next door," the wife replied.

In this case, the husband didn't have to ask why the wife was sarcastic. The reference to the lady next door having the real thing, while she only had imitation, told the whole story.

Phrases That Reveal Positive Feelings

Just as people reveal negative feelings, they also reveal positive feelings by what they say. Sincere compliments, requests for your opinion on important matters, requests for your ideas, and suggestions on personal matters are usually sincere. All of these show respect and trust and are an indication of very positive feelings about you.

An extreme example of an expression of positive feelings is an imitation of the things you do and say. A person who is extremely impressed by you will copy many of your favorite phrases. Dr. Rudolph Flesch says, "Some people go so far in this imitation that in answering the telephone they use the accent of whoever happens to be calling."

The extreme example is rare but does occur. You will more likely encounter imitation of a few phrases, requests for your ideas, opinions, and suggestions. Another indication of positive feelings is listening. If someone you know listens carefully to what you say, he is expressing the highest form of respect and positive feelings.

How Tom Watson Used Conversational Clues to Improve His Popularity

Tom Watson is an intelligent person who often displays creativity and is often very talkative. Tom has travelled throughout the United States, is an avid sports fan, and reads extensively. Consequently Tom is loaded with information. He can talk about any sport, any area of the United States, or any news event of current interest. In spite of all the conversational material at his command, however, Tom was not very popular.

Tom began to notice the verbal and non-verbal clues of the people he talked to after reading a book on non-verbal communication. At first he couldn't understand why people were reacting so negatively to him. After all, he explained, he was very talkative. He always had plenty to talk about and did talk on every occasion. In fact, *that* was the problem. Tom did all the talking and never gave anyone else a chance to say anything.

Once Tom became aware of his unpopular habit, he tried to correct it. Eventually Tom was able to change his overly talkative behavior, and his popularity increased rapidly.

CONVERSATIONAL PLOYS THAT ROOT OUT PEOPLE'S THOUGHTS ABOUT YOU

At one time or another, everyone wonders what other people think about him. This may occur when you first meet someone, when you interview for a job, when you visit new people, when you attend business or social meetings, or when you are caught in an unexpected situation and react differently than you normally would. Techniques have been developed by psychologists and behavioral research scientists that root out or incite expressions of approval or disapproval from other people. I have selected and named two of these to help you find out what people really think about you. I call them the confessional ploy and the false balloon.

The Confessional Ploy

One way to get an acquaintance to open up and reveal his thoughts is to make some small confession. This is an indication that you trust the other person and encourages him to trust you. He or she will feel that if you trust him enough to keep your confession secret, then he can trust you with his comments.

Frank Garland, my friend in California, says "Confession is good because it makes you feel cleansed, even if you're not." Frank said, "I started confessing at an early age." He said he even confessed on his first date. As he tells the story, he was so nervous on his first date that he couldn't say a word. The longer the silence lasted or the more the girl tried to talk to him the more paralyzed Frank became.

Frank kept trying to say something, but just couldn't get it out. Finally he decided to confess his inexperience and tell the girl he would take her home. He blurted out, "I confess," just as the girl had suddenly asked, "Who do you think started the fire in the principal's office, at school?" Frank said he was too embarrassed to correct himself because the girl then confessed to a prank she had pulled on her brother. One confession led to another, and they both kept talking for the rest of the evening.

Frank said the first confession was the best, but he always comes up with a good one when necessary. He says he can always get people to start talking simply by making some small confession.

The False Balloon

The second technique for getting people to reveal their thoughts is to make a false assertion. This is what I call the false balloon. By asserting something that is false to be true, the other person will be encouraged or compelled to correct the statement. Most people are motivated to correct errors or falsehoods. It is much more difficult for people to let a falsehood stand than it is for them to keep a secret.

For example, you might say, "I know talkative people irritate you," even though you know this is not true. The other person will feel compelled to correct your erroneous impression rather than knowingly let you believe something false about himself. The explanation will probably include comments expressing this person's feeling about some things he or she likes or dislikes. You can relate those remarks to the things you do and say to determine how the other person feels about you.

Or, you might relate directly to some personal problem that could possibly irritate the other person. For example, you might say, "I suppose it irritates you when I change the subject so often." If this does irritate the other person, he may respond that "yes" it does irritate him. He will most likely then explain why. He might point out that it is not the change of subject that is irritating, but rather the fact that the other person never gets a chance to comment on the old topic before a new one is introduced. The real thing that is irritating turns out to be the fact that, like most of us, you haven't given the other person an opportunity to comment before changing the subject.

In gaining popularity, of course, it is important to find out the things you do that cause these little irritations. Once you know what they are, you can correct them. Although these irritations are explored fully later, there are two that are so important that they need special attention. They should be worked on constantly in your program of increasing your popularity. One is interrupting the other person, which creates a psychological obstacle in the other person's mind. The second is to speak without pauses. It is very irritating for the listener to not be allowed to make some comment on the topic you are discussing.

Stop interrupting. Since you are the one who is trying to increase your popularity, the burden is on you. You must control your impulse to talk. Often this will be difficult to do; a number of the ideas or opinions expressed by the other person will excite your interest, and that interest will incite the motivational forces within you. You will desire to speak, yet to do so will be an interruption that will irritate the other person and cause him to develop negative feelings about you.

You can stop interrupting, which is a step in developing conversational magic, by remembering to always make sure the other person is through talking before you speak. You can determine this by waiting a second after the other person speaks or by asking "Were you finished?" before you speak. If you err and interrupt someone unintentionally, simply say, "I'm sorry," and stop talking. I can't overstress the importance of not interrupting other people as a basic principal of conversational magic and the development of popularity.

Add pauses to your speech. Not only do we become interested in topics that other people bring up and want to interject our opinion before they finish talking, we also become so interested in our own topic that we try to convey all the information we know before letting the other person speak. This obviously places a burden on the other person. We are asking him to remember each point we bring up, set his response aside, and wait until we cover perhaps five or six points. Then we will permit him to respond, unless we forget and change the subject.

To be a real conversationalist, not just a talker, you need to weave pauses into your speech so the other person has an opportunity to respond to each point. So, make one point at a time. State your point or opinion, pause and let the person comment, then go on to the next point.

In cases where you feel that you must cover two or three points in a row to prove your conclusion, tell the other person what you intend to do. For example, you might say, "Joe, I have three important points to explain the conclusion I've reached. I'd like you to listen to all three and then comment on the three of them." This way you're letting the other person know that he or she will get a chance to talk when you finish the three points. That's conversational magic.

How Jean Branden Used Coversational Ploys to Improve Her Popularity

Jean Branden was hired as a receptionist for the buying office of a large food chain. There were 12 to 15 salespeople in the reception area all the time, which required her to have an outgoing, popular personality. The receptionist was required to log in each salesperson and call the appropriate buyer to notify him of the salesperson's arrival. Often the salesperson would chat with the receptionist while waiting for the buyer to call him in.

One day, Jean's boss called her into his office and told her she was being given two weeks notice. He further advised her that she might consider trying secretarial or some other type work. Jean was completely surprised. She considered herself a good worker and couldn't believe this was happening to her. She asked her boss to explain just what she was doing wrong.

The boss said she just didn't seem to have the personality for the job. He said she was much less popular than the previous receptionist. It wasn't that she didn't do her job, but rather the way she did it. He said she was too curt with people. She acted as though she were doing salespeople a favor by letting them in. "After all," he reminded her, "if not for those salespeople, you wouldn't have a job."

Although Jean was visibly shaken from the bad news, she was determined to do something to correct whatever she was doing wrong. She meant to get the most out of the next two weeks.

Jean began by being more polite to salespeople, and she used conversational ploys to get them to open up. To one she said, "Does it really irritate you when I talk to someone else before I call your buyer." To another she said, "I guess I seem a bit curt at times, when you ask about your appointment." To another, "You seem upset, is it because I answer the phone before giving you the sign-in board?" By using these conversational ploys, Jean was able to get the answers she needed to improve her personality.

As she asked these questions, she also noticed a change in the salespeople. They seemed to be more warm and friendly. She began to talk more to them and they to her. By the end of the two week period, her popularity was on the upswing. She decided to seek a new job as a receptionist now that she knew how to draw people into a conversation and get them to open up through the use of conversational ploys.

3

How to Use Conversational Magic to Develop Poise and Make a Positive Impression

People form impressions of each other within the first ten minutes of conversation. The things you say and the way you say them, during that first ten minutes, determine whether or not you make a positive impression on the people you meet. You can be sure of creating a favorable impression by using the techniques of conversational magic that are explained in this chapter.

You'll learn key conversational phrases that will give you the presence of mind to develop poise, express confidence, and create a positive impression. These key phrases have been helpful, to other people, in overcoming timidity, improving the clarity of their speech and becoming better conversationalists. By using these key techniques, you too can develop poise and make a positive impression.

KEY CONVERSATIONAL PHRASES
THAT INSURE POISE

People judge us both by what we say and by how we say it. They evaluate what we say to determine our educational background, experience, knowledge, ability, and expertise in our particular areas of interest or profession. They evaluate how we speak to determine our enthusiasm, personality, respect, emotional control, and consideration for the needs of others. By using the conversational phrases explained in this section, you can create positive impressions in all these areas of evaluation.

How to Face the World with Poise

There are four easy steps that will help you maintain control and keep your poise in all situations. These steps will help you keep your mental balance, your poise, in conversation. You'll be able to refrain from speaking when you really have nothing to say and be comfortable with silence. You'll develop self-confidence so that in any situation you will be relaxed and speak freely and spontaneously; your poise will show.

I have formed the acronym *FACE* to help you remember the four steps and use them to *face* the world with poise. The four steps are (F) Favorable image phrases, (A) Answering Phrases, (C) Courtroom phrases and (E) Emotional control phrases. All you have to do is remember *FACE* when you are facing a group of new people and you will be able to recall the four steps.

Favorable Image Phrases. (F) To create a favorable image for yourself, you must use phrases that praise or cast a favorable light upon the person you are talking to. You may feel a little awkward during your first few attempts to praise other people, but with practice the awkwardness will disappear. To become poised, you must act poised, and to act poised, you must continually introduce yourself to new people, engage in casual conversation with them, and practice using praise in all your dealings with people.

Praise must be honest and sincere to be effective. People see through insincerity and lose respect for people who praise them when it is not deserved. Fortunately, everyone has something that is praiseworthy. If you look carefully, you will find it. Some men have strong arms and hands and their muscular configuration and size will show this. Some people have artistic hands or make graceful movements. Others have resonant voices or speak in melodious tones. Some are especially good at expressing themselves clearly. Many people are kind, generous unselfish, or considerate of other people's feelings. You can determine which of these favorable traits the person you are speaking with has and praise him for it.

The following phrases are a few of the many you can use to develop a favorable image for yourself while praising other people.

"You seem to have very strong hands."

"Your hands look very artistic, are you an artist or musician?"

"Your voice is very resonant and pleasing."

"Your speech is very melodious."

"Your movements are graceful, are you a dancer?"

"You speak very precisely and clearly."

"You are a kind person."

"You seem very generous."

"You have shown a lot of consideration for other people."

"Your work is neat and well-organized."

"Your suit is very stylish."

"Your tie is really unique."

Answering Questions (A). Many books and articles have been written about asking questions, but answering questions has been completely ignored. The way you answer questions, however, is one of the most important elements of poise and the most critical in forming a positive impression. The way you answer questions reveals your inner feelings, attitudes, assumptions, and sensitivity to the feelings of others. A few well-chosen phrases can keep you off the "hot seat," show that you are warm and considerate, a rational thinking person and a pleasant person to be with.

For example, let's suppose that you are talking to a new friend or a new boss who expresses an opinion in direct conflict with your belief. Your answer is crucial. If you disagree, you may give the impression that you are insentitive to or inconsiderate of the opinions of others. On the other hand, if you violate your own integrity and pretend to agree with an opinion you really oppose, you may wind up with a more serious problem. Many people will easily see through your pretense, and you may find yourself continually defending a position you disagree with. How long can you remember which side you're on with whom?

The problem can be resolved by finding a polite phrase that changes your answer from an evaluation of the other person to an honest expression of your own feelings or opinion. You always have the right and owe it to yourself—to preserve your integrity—to honestly express your own opinion. A friend of mine has found a phrase that adequately resolves the problem. When someone expresses an opinion that he disagrees with, he simply says, *"I don't share that opinion."* This magic phrase, "I don't share that opinion," is not critical of the other person and is not a sell-out of your integrity. It builds respect and leaves a positive impression.

People often ask personal questions through ignorance or brashness. Again, you leave a better impression if you answer without evaluating the person who asked the question. The fact that the other person is rude or ill-mannered does not justify a sarcastic or rude answer. Remember, no matter what the question, your poise and the impression you make will depend upon the way you answer.

One way to answer a personal question without being rude or sarcastic is to act as though only part of the answer is personal (indicating the questioner might not have known). This takes the pressure off the questioner, shows that you can retain your poise under adverse conditions, and retains the confidentiality of personal information.

Some examples of answers that deal with personal questions are:

"I'm sorry, but to answer that question I would have to break a confidence."

"I'm sorry, part of the answer contains confidential information."

"I can't answer you completely without revealing confidental information."

"I'm sorry, the answer would contain personal information that pertains to someone else."

"The best answer I can give, without revealing information, is . . ."

"It is difficult to answer that question without revealing confidential information."

"It is difficult to answer your question because part of the answer contains information about someone else that I've been asked not to reveal."

Courtroom Phrases That Build Respect (C). The phrases people use in a courtroom are usually overly polite. Especially polite are the phrases that are used when addressing the judge. There is some justification for showing the same courtesy to everyone you meet as you would a judge. After all, courtesy is simply a mark of respect. Everyone is entitled to respect for his or her character and sensitivity for others rather than his position. The way to always retain your poise and make a positive impression is to always talk as though you were in a courtroom speaking to a judge. For example you might say, "If it pleases you" (If it pleases the court), or "If you approve" (If the court approves).

Emotional Control (E). Emotional control, the fourth and final step in maintaining control and developing poise, is control of your own emotions. By keeping your emotions under control, you avoid emotional outbreaks, sarcasm, and illogical remarks that would leave a negative impression. The following five points will help you control your emotions.

1. *Realize that you can be more effective if you do control your emotions.* If you've ever watched someone else become emotional and shout, curse, or cry, you can easily

realize that to retain poise and give a positive impression, you must control your emotions. If you've ever watched a person try to make a point or express an opinion when he was angry, you probably noticed that he just irritated others, which made it impossible to make his point. If you want people to see you as a logical, rational person, control your emotions.

2. *Know that you can control your own emotions.* You don't have to get mad or lose control of your emotions. It is well documented by psychological research that people can raise their tolerance of frustration. You can retain your poise and control your emotions simply by recognizing your tolerance level and working to keep your cool when frustrating events occur.

3. *Make a list of the things that irritate you.* You can more easily learn to control your emotions if you prepare in advance to deal with the things that irritate you. Keep a record for six months of all the things that irritate you. Group these irritations in classes, and list them in a notebook or keep them on a sheet of paper where you can review them daily. By checking the list daily, you can think about how you will deal with irritating events without losing control of your emotions.

4. *Look at anger-provoking situations as ironic trivialties of life.* No matter how well we plan, we often face obstacles that ironically interfere with our plans. We practice until we reach a stage of near perfection, and the event we practiced for is cancelled. A man executes a perfect bank robbery and gets trapped in the vault. We buy stocks, and the market goes down. Or we accept a higher paying job in a distant city, and when we get there find that the cost of living is so high that we wind up with less disposable income than we had prior to the promotion. Those are examples of the ironic trivialities of life.

   Become aware of the irony of these trivialities and realize that we can't do anything about them. The best we can ever do is to plan for future events, try to prepare for any eventuality, and then do the best we can under whatever circumstances arise. We cannot help matters by becoming angry, so we might as well learn to keep cool.

5. *Laugh at those trivialities and at your tendency to let them control your emotions.* Research has shown that we can't express anger and laughter at the same time. So if you can find humor in the situation and laugh at it, you won't become angry and lose control of your emotions. We Americans pride ourselves on our freedom from control, yet we often let people and events control us by irritating us until we lose control of our own emotions and react in anger.

Learn to laugh at the irony in the situation when some unexpected event interferes with your plan. Remember to look for something to laugh at first. If you can't find any humor in the situation, then think of something humorous that occurred in the past and laugh at it. Recreating the humor from the past will keep you from losing control of your emotions. You simply won't get mad while you're laughing or smiling. Each time you overcome your tendency to get angry, you raise your tolerance level. Eventually you will be able to control your emotions and retain your poise in all situations. Remember that these irritating problems will arise when you are not expecting them and when you are least prepared to deal with them. So when the unexpected occurs, say to yourself, "I've got to smile." Then stall for time by asking a question until you can regain your poise.

Two of My Friends Use Humor to Retain Control of Their Emotions

I have two friends whose easy conversational style draws attention like magic. Although they don't know each other, they share the experience of having overcome a hostile background and becoming humorists rather than emotionally controlled angry people. Reed, from Missouri, was raised in extreme poverty and was belittled and browbeaten by other children in the neighborhood. Mort from Texas, was abused physically by an uncaring parent.

Both Reed and Mort suffered many traumatic experiences as children and might have reacted by forming hostile attitudes and turning against their fellow man as criminals. Neither did.

These two friends of mine developed a humorous approach to life and thus overcame the environment that could have molded them into hostile people who could not control their own emotions.

Both Reed, from Missouri and Mort from Texas, although they have never met, share a common approach to life. They share the homespun philosophy of Will Rogers, the humor of Billy Carter, and the poise and sophistication of Johnny Carson. They are similar in their easy, humorous reactions to challenges or problems. They love life and see humor in every experience. They love people and share in the delight of entertaining others. They also share in the joy of their individual brand of poise, popularity, and success they have gained from their own brand of conversational magic.

Mort and Reed, both conditioned to facing unreasonable people, have learned to reason in all situations. They still face economic, social, and psychological barriers in their careers, but they overcome these formidible barriers by quick-witted, good-natured conversational magic. They have learned to control their emotions by always finding humor in the ironic trivialities of life.

KEY PHRASES THAT CREATE
POSITIVE IMPRESSIONS

To give a positive impression, you must speak positively, act positively, and react positively to suggestions, criticism, and ideas. The easiest way to accomplish your objective is to learn some key phrases that give a favorable impression. As you use these phrases, you will begin to think and act more positively.

To create a positive impression, show that you are enthusiastic, respectful, intellectual, an expert, courteous, interesting, have high moral values, and are willing to learn from others. The following sets of phrases will accomplish this purpose.

1. Phrases That Create Enthusiasm
2. Phrases That Show Respect
3. Phrases That Reveal Your Expertise
4. Phrases That Build Your Intellectual Image
5. Phrase That Add Interest to Your Speech

Phrases That Create Enthusiasm

Phrases that create enthusiasm are those that promise positive results, rewards, or a general feeling of well being. The following examples may be used to create enthusiasm for the situation indicated.

For New Ideas

"It sounds great."
"I think it will work."
"I know you're on to a good thing."
"I'm sure you'll succeed."
"I can see you'll do it."
"I think you can do it."

To Get People to Change

"You'll like it better."
"You'll have more friends."
"Everyone will see how well you're doing."
"You'll make more money."
"You'll be more secure."
"You'll learn new skills."
"You'll get to try your own ideas."

To Create a General Feeling of Well Being

"I feel great."
"I'm doing extremely well."
"Everyone is doing well."
"Things couldn't be better."

Phrases That Show Respect

Phrases that show respect are those that ask for the other person's opinion or comment favorably on his or her past performance.

Asking for Opinions

"What do you think of . . .?"
"How do you feel about . . .?"
"What is your opinion on . . .?"

"What do you suggest . . .?"
"How would you handle . . .?"

Commenting on Past Performance

"You handled the complaint in a professional way."
"Your results show how well you did your job."
"Your productivity has increased."
"You handle people well."
"That statement to your subordinate shows that you
   know how to handle people."

Phrases That Reveal Your Expertise

Everyone is an expert at something, but we usually become
so involved in doing it that we forget our level of expertise. All
you have to do is look at your job, your hobbies, or your social activities to determine where you have the most expertise. Then
review the basics and write out your own phrases that will reveal
your expertise.

Research has shown that people who are considered experts
in their field often differ widely in the actual knowledge they
hold. They gained their reputation as an expert not by their
superior knowledge but rather by how they used it. Three
characteristics that are most often associated with experts are:
(1) the publication of a magazine article, (2) a speech at a public
gathering, or (3) the development of a new innovation. The key
to the first two obviously is the development of phrases that
reveal the expertise in an interesting way.

The way to develop interesting phrases that reveal your expertise is to turn complicated professional terms into under-
standable language by connecting basic definitions with words
such as *secret, reveal, complications, inside,* etc. For example,
the following phrases reveal how experts explain their complicated material to laymen.

"The secret of Industrial Advertising is . . . "
"Now I'll reveal the background story on . . . "
"To explain the complications involved, I'll use this
   basic model."

"The inside approach to this problem is to . . ."

Phrases such as those listed above can be used in magazine articles or in speeches to develop interest. At the same time, you appear to be the expert who is revealing, explaining, telling the secret or giving inside information. These phrases can help develop your image as an expert and help create a positive impression that will enhance your popularity and lead to success.

Phrases That Build Your Intellectual Image

In building an intellectual image, you must be very cautious. It is better to forget about building an intellectual image than to turn off all your friends in the process. If you seem to be arrogant or egotistical, you will lose rather than gain popularity. If you have any problem in this area now, it is better to try to correct the problem before trying to build an intellectual image.

An intellectual image should be built slowly. What you want is the image of a quiet intellectual rather than the loud preacher.

As a quiet intellectual, you must always speak politely and with restraint. Never become loud and obnoxious, but speak firmly and with conviction. Raise your voice to make a point and use inflections to add interest to your speech. Never argue or become emotional. If you can't convince the person to whom you are talking to accept your point of view, spend your time trying to understand his point of view. That alone will convince him that you are overly intelligent.

Although you must wait for an opportunity to use them, you can develop modern phrases that show intellectual insight by rephrasing an old allegory, anecdote or parable in modern terms. For example, you might rephrase "When it rains it pours," by using dust instead of rain. You might say, "Bringing up and old argument is like stirring up a dust storm. The more dirt you throw, the dirtier you get."

You can take any old parable or allegory and do the same thing with it. First determine its meaning, find a new modern medium to carry the message, then rewrite it in modern terms. Develop a number of these modern phrases and have them ready to use when the proper occasion arises.

Phrases That Add Interest to Your Speech

The way to add interest to your speech is to describe some benefit for the other person. For example, you might point out that what you have to say will help the listener in some way. The information might help them become better adjusted, meet new people, become financially secure or feel better about themselves.

The value in stating these benefits is two-fold, you get attention and you remind your listener that a specific action will result in a specific benefit. By learning conversational techniques, for example, you will be more popular with people. You can tie in to the following phrases with your topic of conversation

"This . . . will give you more security."
"This . . . will make you more popular."
"This . . . will increase your finances."
"This . . . will gain new respect for you."
"This . . . will be a challenge for you."
"This . . . will give you more prestige."
"This . . . will give you more recognition."

How a Shy Student Underwent a Magical Change and Made a Positive Impression

Jerry Mandel was a shy student who had very few friends. Jerry felt badly about himself and was very negative in his speech and in his approach to life. Jerry met a girl whom he liked very much, but she could not stand his negative attitude. When Jerry found this was the problem, he became very upset and decided to do something about his negative approach to life.

Jerry had a counsellor help him develop a plan to change his image. Jerry first worked on his response to greetings. When asked, "How are you?" Jerry would respond positively with "fine" or "great." When listening to the ideas and opinions of others, he would try to find something positive to comment on. He refused to make a negative comment about anything, and slowly his own attitude began to change.

Jerry developed a number of positive phrases to fit any situation that came up; soon his popularity began to grow. As he became more popular and gained new friends, his positive approach became natural for him. He forgot the reason for changing because he became too busy with his new-found popularity to think about it.

4

How to Start Conversations with Friends or Strangers

Starting a conversation is difficult only when you are unaware of the interests of the person you are trying to converse with. In most cases you don't know the interests of strangers, therefore, you have difficulty in speaking to them. In many cases, you feel some nervousness and this also interferes with your attempts at conversation.

Conversations with friends are usually much easier because you know their interests. Occasionally, however, you may have talked out the usual topics of interest, and conversation drags even with friends. In those situations where you lack a conversational topic, either with friends or strangers, you can use the techniques revealed in this chapter to find an area of interest.

This chapter starts with ten easy ways to start a conversation. Then special areas that interest women are covered, followed by special areas that interest men. Finally, special techniques and examples are used to illustrate holding conversations with men and women.

TEN EASY WAYS TO START A CONVERSATION

I have selected ten topics that are often found in everyday conversation. These topics are based in psychology. They relate to people's internal drives to enhance their personality, and provide ten easy ways to start a conversation. The ten topics listed below are tied in to memory clues in the paragraphs that follow and describe them.

1. Ask a Background Question
2. Comment on a Local Event
3. Pay a Compliment
4. Ask for Advice
5. Find Something to Praise
6. Ask for Help
7. Ask for an Opinion
8. Ask for an Evaluation
9. Ask About Local Customs
10. Ask About Local Restaurants

Conversation Starter #1

The first conversation starter, *Ask a Background Question,* is the most often used. By asking a background question, you draw out information about the other person that provides a starting point for conversation. The background information may pertain to the other person's state of origin, schools attended, previous work, hobbies, friends, family, or social or professional background. Whatever the information revealed, it will be about and of interest to the person revealing the information. It provides, therefore, an interesting topic of conversation.

An interesting way to remember the conversation starters is to tie each one in to a memory clue. The clue that I use for number one is a large mental map of the United States. This map becomes the background and reminds me to ask a question about the other person's state of origin. I can then locate them on the map. I actually visualize them standing on this giant map in the state of their origin. Once I have them located on the map, it is easy to continue the conversation by asking for information about the state or about family members who might still be living there.

Conversation Starter #2

The second conversation starter, *Comment on a Local Event* follows naturally from the first. You started with a picture of the United States; now you are going to narrow that down to a local event. This could either be a political, sports, or any other local event. The clue I use to remember this conversation starter is a political speaker, perhaps the town mayor, in a black silk top hat. I picture him making a speech at a football stadium. This reminds me that there are all kinds of different events (political, sports, etc.) to comment on.

Your comment may grow out of something the other person said in response to your background question. The other person may show an interest in sports, for example. You can then tie that interest in to local sports.

If the other person comments on a sport that you are unfamiliar with, explain that you don't follow that sport and then ask for some information about it. Never dismiss or ignore a topic brought up by the other person. In doing so you give the impression that you are self-centered and only interested in your own topics of conversation. Let the other person talk his topic out before changing the subject.

Conversation Starter #3

Conversation starter number three is to *Pay a Compliment.* I remember number three by picturing myself placing a ribbon with three medals on it around the mayor's neck. It's a little problem getting it over the top hat of course, but that reminds me that compliments can backfire if they are insincere. People see through insincere compliments and will not be likely to converse very long with an insincere person.

There are always a number of things for which people deserve sincere compliments. Perhaps one article of clothing is especially nice or perhaps different articles of clothing are well matched. The personal qualities of voice, complexion, hands, fingers, artistic movements, etc., are all there awaiting your compliment. If you look for things to compliment people on, you will find them in abundance.

You may feel somewhat timid at first, but you will overcome this very rapidly. Make certain your compliments are sincere and practice giving compliments every day. You may have to force yourself at first, but the rewards of warm appreciation and friendly conversation will soon help you overcome your nervousness and timidity.

Conversation Starter #4

One way to keep a conversation going forever is to use conversation starter number four, *Ask for Advice.* It's good as a conversation starter and is very useful in keeping a conversation going. I remember this "starter" by handing our imaginary mayor four microphones. Two for each hand. Politicians love to give advice, and with four microphones they can give all the advice they want. By forming this vivid picture of a mayor making a speech with four microphones in his hands, I am always able to remember to ask for advice to start or keep a conversation going.

Just as praise must be sincere, so should seeking advice. There are any number of things you can legitimately ask advice about. If you have found or know about certain areas the other person has expertise in, then ask for advice in those areas. Not only does asking for advice keep the conversation going, it also shows respect for the other person. It shows that you value his knowledge and experience.

For example, if you find that the other person is a carpenter, you might ask his advice on building your own house or building an extra room or some other project. Or you might ask his advice on purchasing your own tools—What tools would be best for the job. The more detail you ask for, the longer the conversation lasts, the more you learn, and the better you become in conversation.

Conversation Starter #5

Conversation starter number five is to *Find Something to Praise.* This doesn't have to be praise for the person you are talking to; it can be praise for anyone or anything. The idea is to bring excitement and exuberance into the conversation. Everyone likes to hear interesting stories and by praising someone or something, you are telling a story. The more aspects to your praise, the more detailed and interesting the story becomes.

Don't try the same thing with criticism or complaints, it won't work. No one wants to hear a lot of complaints or derogatory remarks about other people. That takes out the interest that praise builds in. It is also wise to avoid praising members of your own family. That story has already been told by someone else. Only when talking to very close friends or other members of the family is it good taste to praise family members.

I remember praise, the fifth conversation starter, by thinking of the five vowels, a, e, i, o, and u. To pronounce those vowels correctly is worthy of praise. If you realize that people who speak with accents differ in their speech primarily by the way they pronounce vowels, you can see that pronouncing these five vowels correctly is worthy of praise.

You may wish to develop your own memory clues to help recall the conversational starters. I use the ones I have developed and explained in this book because they are easy for me as they relate to personal experiences. Since we all differ in background and experience, you might develop more meaningful clues for your own use.

If you do develop your own personal clues, make them vivid. Exaggerate them, form them out of proportion with their surroundings or blend them into some strong or unusual action such as an explosion, breaking apart or crashing into something. The more vivid you make the picture, the more easily you will be able to recall it.

Conversation Starter #6

Ask for Help is the sixth conversation starter. Everyone responds to helping others, in most instances, because it appeals not only to their humanitarian instincts but also to their ego. To ask for help, implies the person asked is intelligent enough, caring enough, or strong enough to provide the help asked for.

I remember this easily by imagining myself at the bottom of a six foot ladder, that I have fallen from; A bucket of brand "6" paint is falling toward me from the top of the ladder. I, of course, am yelling "help."

Conversation Starter #7

The seventh conversation starter is to *Ask for an Opinion.* This is the easiest of all because there are millions of things to ask opinions on, and most people are just waiting for a chance to give them. When you ask someone to give you an opinion, you are saying you respect his judgment, you are interested in what he has to say, and you believe his opinion is important. In other words, you see him as being important and worthy of your attention.

I remember starter number seven by picturing a mailbox on a post. The mailbox and the post together form a "seven." I picture the mailbox opened with a stack of letters inside; each of the letters is stamped, Opinion Survey. As soon as I visualize the word opinion on the letters, I remember to ask for an opinion.

Conversation Starter #8

Conversational starter number eight is the most difficult of all. It is not appropriate when conversing with strangers, but works well with friends, family, and superiors at work. Number eight is to *Ask for an Evaluation.* The reason this is so difficult is that when you ask for an evaluation, you will most likely get criticism. Criticism is difficult for many people to take. They feel they are being personally attacked or ridiculed.

Poor feelings about criticism result from two factors: (1) most people don't give criticism properly, and (2), we feel criticism makes us look stupid or unintelligent. We therefore, fight, argue, and reject criticism in order to retain our false image of infallibility.

To grow as human beings, we must be evaluated, we must get criticism. If we don't, we remain at a very immature psychological age while our friends—who are getting criticism—are growing, becoming more mature, and leaving us behind. The answer, of course, is that we must seek evaluation. We must learn to accept criticism and correct the errors or make the improvements the evaluation calls for.

I remember number eight by thinking of two revolving doors, one opening into the other. I go around one, exit into the other, go around the second, and exit back into the first. Obviously, that kind of activity requires some criticism. It reminds me to ask for an evaluation periodically to find out how I'm doing.

Conversational Starter #9

Conversational starter number nine is to *Ask About Local Customs.* If you are a stranger in town, you can ask about the customs of the town you are in. If not and you are speaking to someone from some other location, then ask about the customs of the town or city that person is from. You can then compare the customs of the stranger's town to those of your own.

This may lead to other comparisons between the two towns. Differences between towns, expecially historical aspects, are always interesting; you will find one topic developing into another and another and another. Soon you will wonder where all the time went, and how you could have talked so long.

I remember number nine by thinking of an old mine. The mine rhymes with nine and is recallable by number nine, just as number eight will recall the revolving doors which form a figure eight when connected to each other. In front of the mine, I form a picture of a small group of people sitting around a campfire swapping stories about their home towns. This reminds me to ask about local customs.

Conversational Starter #10

Conversational starter number ten, a pleasant one, is to *Ask About Local Restaurants.* Food obviously appeals to everyone and everyone, consequently, is interested in restaurants. This is a topic that can lead to a conversation that can run for an hour. It can be discussed in any city in the world and provides a worldwide common area of interest.

Asking about restaurants also gives the other person an opportunity to show what he knows about his city. The topic can easily be switched to theater or other forms of public entertainment.

I remember conversations starter number ten, simply by thinking a large "10" attached to the top of a restaurant. I then think of my ten favorite restaurants in my home city. This reminds me to ask the other person to tell me about *his* favorite restaurants.

How to Use the Ten Conversation Starters

The ten conversation starters should be memorized by tying them in to the memory clues, but need not be used in numerical order. Using them in order during your early attempts at opening conversations is acceptable as a method of memorization. After you gain familiarity with the conversation starters then switch to a random method of using them. If you start with number one, jump to number seven, then back to number two, etc., your conversation will seem more spontaneous and interesting.

Remember that conversational starters are only meant to get the conversation opened. After it is opened, spontaneous give-and-take will carry the conversation forward. Should the conversation wane and not develop from continued attempts with alternate conversation starters, then a more strategic approach should be taken to sustain conversation.

Conversational Strategy

A conversational strategy is one that leads to a specific goal. For example, you might set as your goal to learn about the economic base of the community where your conversational partner lives. By keeping this goal in mind, you can constantly direct the conversation toward those elements and details of a community that relate to its economic base.

You may ask a sequence of questions that lead from a general overview of the community to a more and more detailed examination of a wide variety of elements that affect the economy of the community. This examination will provide an unending source of conversational topics.

HOW TO TALK TO WOMEN ABOUT THE TOPICS THAT INTEREST THEM MOST

Some men find it difficult to converse with women. This problem arises when men are not aware of the things that women find most interesting. This is less of a problem today and will continue to be reduced in the future as women become more interested in sports and occupations historically reserved to men.

Five Conversational Topics That Interest Women

To enable men to overcome their difficulty in talking to women, I have developed a list of the five things that women find most interesting. An initial survey of 500 women resulted in over thirty specific items. These items were grouped into similar classes. For example, sports, fishing movies, reading, etc. were all grouped under the group "Recreation." An additional 350 women were then asked to rank the groups with the #1 being the most interesting, #2 the next most interesting, etc.

The topic most interesting to most women. The topic that most women ranked #1 was "family and home." This topic was ranked #1 by nearly 200 of the 350 women who answered the survey questions. Most of the women who did not rank "family and home" number one, ranked it two or three. All the ranking numbers were added and averaged. "Family and home" averaged 1.5 which is the highest ranking any item received.

The women who answered the questionaire were general office workers, secretaries, and school teachers. Slight differences in ranking may be found between specifically identifiable separate groups of women. Single women for example, in the preliminary questioning period, mentioned men more often than did married women.

The second most interesting topic to women. The topic selected as the second most interesting to the 350 women surveyed was "friends." In the initial questioning of the first 500 women, "friends" or "friendship" ranked in second place also. It was very clear from our research that women from all walks of life consider their friends or their friendships to be interesting and a most important factor in their lives.

The third most interesting topic to women. The topic that women rated as their third most interesting was their own personal growth. Since all the respondents in our study were working women, it would be interesting to compare this finding with a survey of non-working women. This is consistent with the verbally expressed desires of women to seek more responsible positions both at the local and national level.

Discussions with the women respondents revealed that personal growth was not necessarily a goal to achieve success in the business world, but rather a sincere desire to improve as a person. If success on the job came as a result of this improvement, it would be accepted. The real purpose of personal growth, however, was the personal satisfaction of accomplishment.

The fourth most interesting topic to women. The topic ranked fourth, by the women in the survey, was "good health." Although this topic may have limited conversational value, it is interesting to know that women ranked it so high. Conversation might be directed at activities and foods that promote good health rather than the state of health of any particular person.

The fifth most interesting topic to women. The women responding in this survey ranked "work or job" as the fifth most interesting topic. Work, of course, offers an endless stream of conversational topics. You can ask questions relating to how people feel about their work or about the specific details of the work itself. Once any mention of work is made, it triggers numerous thoughts of things that happen on the job and leads to hours of conversation.

Other Topics That Interest Women

All the topics mentioned by the 500 women in the initial study were combined into fourteen groups. Those groups are listed below in order as ranked by the women in the study.

1. Family and Home
2. Friends
3. Personal Growth
4. Good Health
5. Work or Job
6. Recreation
7. Travel
8. National News
9. Material Wealth
10. Local News
11. Psychology
12. Religion
13. Shopping
14. Clothes

How a Shy Accountant Became Popular with Women

Tom Hartman, a shy accountant, overcame his inability to talk to women by using the conversational starters and discussing the topics of interest that were determined in this study. Tom kept the list of fourteen topics on a small card in his pocket. He would use one of the conversation starters to engage a woman in conversation; then he would follow up by asking questions about the topics of interest listed on his card.

Tom would, for example, ask about the lady's home and family. This normally would elicit a great deal of information. Tom would intersperse comments about his own family and home and continue the conversation to its conclusion.

When this topic was exhausted, Tom would simply move to another item on the list. He might ask, "How do you like your work?" Or, "How do you feel about the national news report on . . .?" Tom not only overcame his shyness, he also became a very popular, sought-after conversationalist.

HOW TO TALK TO MEN ABOUT THE TOPICS THAT INTEREST THEM MOST

Remember that in conversations with men or women, these topics of interest are used to start and keep a conversation going. In utilizing conversational magic, you must also remember to show courtesy, display poise, and be friendly. And most importantly, listen and don't interrupt when the other person is talking.

The Five Conversational Topics That Are Most Interesting to Men

The topics found to be more interesting to men in our first study were:

1. Family and home
2. Self-improvement
3. Work or Job
4. Recreation
5. Travel

The same techniques that were used to determine the topics of interest for women were used to determine those of men. First the men were asked to list five topics of interest; then these topics were grouped and formed into fewer categories so they could be further ranked by men in the study. The following list of topics are ranked in their order of interest as selected by the men in the study.

The topic most interesting to most men. Men chose family and home as their most interesting topic. A revealing aspect of this study was that single as well as married men ranked family and home as their number one area of interest. Evidently family ties are stronger than the news media often lead us to believe.

In any event, it is certain that both men and women will be interested in and respond to questions or comments about their families. Since this topic holds universal interest, it would be appropriate to start conversations with strangers by asking questions such as, "Do you have a family here?" Or, "Is your family in this area?" Any question relating to the family that is not of a personal nature and respects the dignity of the family is appropriate.

The second most interesting topic to men. In our initial studies, we asked men to list the five topics that interested them the most. We gave no clues, no definitions and only minor explanations as to what we wanted. Our basic explanation was, "anything in the world that interests you." We felt the less explanation we gave, the more honest and spontaneous the results would be.

This led to some differences in the words men used from those used by women. The topic selected as the second most interesting to men was "self-improvement." Women, on the other hand said "personal growth" to express this area of interest. This difference suggests a wide area of exploration possibilities. In conversation you can ask questions to explore these differences. For example, you might refer to this study and pose the question, "Do you feel there is a difference in 'self-improvement' and 'personal growth'?" Or, "Doesn't 'self-improvement' imply you have to do it yourself while 'personal growth' may simply result from external factors?" You can see the possibilities for conversation here are endless.

The third most interesting topic to men. Men overwhelmingly selected "work or job" as their third most interesting topic. A few people in the study ranked work below three but no one ranked it lower than six. The implication is clear—men are very highly involved in and interested in their work. A comment or question about their work will generally result in a long and probably interesting conversation about their job, company, other people in the company and their own career plans. Each of these areas can be expanded by further questioning.

The fourth most interesting topic to men. Men selected "recreation" as their fourth most interesting topic. The word recreation was used in the second phase of the study to encompass all the various words the men had used in the initial study. Worlds like sports, fishing, football, reading, movies, etc., used by the men in the first study were grouped into the "recreation" classification for the second study. Again, the conversational possibilities are endless. Just a few opening questions, for example, could lead to hours of interesting conversation. For example:

Question: "What is your favorite sport?"
Answer: "Hockey"
Comment: "Oh! I know nothing about hockey. Could you
          tell me a little about it?"
Reply: "Sure . . . ."

By asking for further information, for clarification, opinions, and examples, this conversation can go on for hours. In the process, you will gain valuable information that will enhance your own conversational ability when you next meet someone interested in hockey.

The fifth most interesting topic to men. Men selected travel as their fifth most interesting topic. The study did not attempt to determine whether they actually liked to travel themselves or simply found it interesting as a topic of conversation. The allure of visiting new cities either in our own or foreign countries has been frequently documented and offers an excellent topic of conversation.

Differences in Men and Women's Areas of Interests

There were some minor differences found in the ranked interests of men and women. Since our study of women had been much more comprehensive, we considered it valid and reliable. Our study of men however, covered only a small group of business men and was not statistically valid or reliable. We did run a third small sample survey of men and found our results reliable for businessmen, but again our sample was not statistically significant.

We decided to give the men the list previously ranked by women and have the men rank the topics on the women's list. From that ranking we found that men changed their top five topics of interest to (1) family and home, (2) good health, (3) work or job, (4) personal growth, and (5) friends. The introduction of the "good health" classification seems to be responsible for the change in the men's ranking.

The following lists compare the rankings of 14 items by men and women.

Topics Ranked in Order of Highest Interest by:

WOMEN	MEN
1. Family and Home	1. Family and Home
2. Friends	2. Good Health
3. Personal Growth	3. Work or Job
4. Good Health	4. Personal Growth
5. Work or Job	5. Friends
6. Recreation	6. Recreation
7. Travel	7. Material Wealth
8. National News	8. Religion
9. Material Wealth	9. Travel
10. Local News	10. National News
11. Psychology	11. Clothes
12. Religion	12. Psychology
13. Shopping	13. Local News
14. Clothes	14. Shopping

How a Young Woman Used Topics Interesting to Men to Improve Her Poise and Popularity

Sherri Lane felt nervous and ill at ease around men. She constantly lost her poise, was afraid to attend social gatherings for fear of "putting her foot in her mouth" as she described it, and was unhappy because (as she said) she was not popular at all. I suggested that Sherri memorize the topics that were most interesting to men and then practice them.

Sherri memorized the five topics and forced herself to attend social gatherings. At first Sherri meekly asked such questions as,

> "Do you have a family here?"
> "What interests do you have in self-improvement?"
> "What are the most rewarding aspects of your work?"
> "What do you do for recreation?"
> "Do you travel often?"

She listened to their answers but didn't really add anything to the conversation. But she soon learned to offer comments, evaluations, and opinions on what was said. In a few months, she felt comfortable in any social situation, and as she loosened up and talked openly, her popularity began to grow. She is now a happy, popular conversationalist who has successfully used conversational magic with both friends and strangers to win poise, popularity, and success.

5

How to Use Psychological Techniques to Put Magic into Your Conversation

One way to develop conversational magic is to use psychological techniques that gain people's interest and attention. Research in recent years has identified the basic psychological elements of a conversation. These elements as well as other psychological techniques will be revealed in this chapter.

You will also learn, in this chapter, how to deal with feelings of inferiority, to clear away emotional barriers, to stand up to overpowering people, and to develop conversational techniques to keep control of the conversation. The techniques revealed in this chapter will provide the psychological base upon which you can develop your own style of conversational magic.

THE SECRET OF BEING AN INTERESTING CONVERSATIONALIST

There are nine basic psychological techniques that add interest, gain trust, create psychological obligations, determine good timing, and help you determine your impact on other people. These techniques are:

1. Create a Psychological Obligation
2. Have Empathy
3. Respond to Emotion
4. Respond to Excitement
5. Recognize Irrational Actions
6. Use an Interest Facilitator
7. Ask Functional Questions
8. Check Your Timing
9. Measure Your Impact

Create a Psychological Obligation

To create a psychological obligation on the part of another person, you must provide an equal courtesy to that person. If, for example, you want someone to listen carefully to what you say without criticism, then you must first listen to him without criticism. If you want people to help you, then you must offer to help them. If you want people to try your ideas, you must express your willingness to try their ideas. If you want people to excuse your errors, then you must, when they occur, excuse the errors of other people.

Not only do these courteous actions build an equal or like psychological obligation, they also have a cumulative effect. If you use them all without concern for whether or not you are creating a single psychological obligation, you soon find that you have built a generalized psychological obligation similar to that of friendship. To create this generalized psychological obligation and add interest to your conversation, remember to:

a. Listen to other people without criticism.
b. Offer to help others when help is needed
c. Be willing to try the other person's ideas.
d. Excuse other people's errors as being human.

Have Empathy

Empathy is so rare that it is valued above all other human traits. Most people do not try to really understand the other person's feelings, problems, and point of view. Dr. Carl Rogers found that, to really help his emotionally disturbed patients, he had to understand the framework that his patients' thoughts and feelings evolved from. In other words, he had to mentally stand in the shoes of the patient. Then he could show real understanding and human compassion.

This approach taken by Dr. Rogers won the interest and trust of his patients. They began to listen more and clarify their own ideas and respond with an empathy of their own toward him. Dr. Rogers later demonstrated to a meeting of the American Psychological Association that the same techniques worked as well with average people in social conversation. By having empathy with your friends and acquaintances, you can gain their trust and hold their interest in conversation.

Respond to Emotions

When someone expresses an emotion such as sorrow or anger, respond to that emotion. Let the other person know that you recognize the sorrow or anger or fear he feels. Say, "You seem to be upset, tell me what's wrong." After he tells you what's bothering him, express understanding. Say, "I can understand your being upset under those conditions." By responding to emotions in this way, you help the other person work through his difficulties. He then sees you as an interesting and helpful person.

Use an Interest Facilitator

An interest facilitator is a sentence or phrase that holds promise of a benefit to the other person. The benefit can be money, happiness, friends, security, or respect. Anything that promises a benefit catches the other person's attention and interest. You can determine what benefit to mention by analyzing his interests.

Since people generally talk about the things that interest them, you need only listen to your conversational partner talk a few times to determine these interests. Then you mention a benefit that relates to one of his areas of interest. This will gain his interest and attention.

Ask Functional Questions

Functional questions are used to determine the mood, responsiveness, or friendliness of the other person. The only way to find these answers is to ask the other person. Generally, when asked they will tell you themselves. To determine the mood, ask the other person how he or she feels about some happy occasion. Perhaps you can relate to a home team's winning game. If the other person is in a good mood, his or her response will be cheerful. If moody, the answer will reflect it.

A question or comment about the weather will result in a friendly and responsive comment if the other person feels friendly and responsive. If the response is not friendly, it is best to move on to someone else for the time being to give the first person time to improve his mood and feelings.

Recognize Irrational Actions

You obviously can't be interesting to someone who is so confused or upset as to be irrational. If someone starts to act in irrational ways, the best policy is to remain quiet and keep a safe distance from him. If you pay attention to what people say, you will learn to recognize even the more subtle irrational actions.

An inappropriate remark, sarcasm, belittling others, or undue forgiveness for a wrong may be irrational. The more open indications of irrationality often accompany anger. Verbal threats accompanied by clenched fists and a reddened face are irrational, and so are ranting, raving and physical attacks.

Irrational actions are usually the result of some vividly imagined or real danger. Irrational people are dangerous because they are responding automatically and unconsciously to a perceived threat to their lives. Stay out of their way.

Respond to Excitement

One of the best ways to win friendship is to appreciate and share in the excitement of others. If someone shows that he is excited, respond to that excitement. Say, "Hey, you really are excited. Tell me all about it." Then make comments to show that you share the excitement. As the person explains say, "That's great," or "Wow," or whatever you feel. It doesn't matter what you say, just show excitement when you say it.

Timing Tip-offs

In the book *How to Use Psychological Leverage to Double the Power of What You Say,* (Parker Publishing Company, Inc.,

1978), I coined three terms to describe the tip-offs people give that tell you your timing is right. These terms are:

1. Incremental Uncertainty
2. Segmented Approval
3. Questions of Interest

The first tip-off, *Incremental Uncertainty*, is a statement indicating the other person does not have a fixed position. In effect, he says, "I'm willing to listen." This tip-off is expressed with statements such as, "I don't know," "Maybe," "I'm not sure," "I don't think so."

The second tip-off, *Segmented Approval,* is a statement that approves a part or segment of what you've said. This person may have previously disagreed with everything you've said but is now more receptive because he finally saw the logic in one small segment of your remarks. Segmented approval is expressed with statements such as, "That one point seems right." "I think the first part of your idea is right." "Part of what you say is true."

The third and most definite tip-off is *Questions of Interest.* Questions for more information or additional details are sure signs that your timing is right. If the other person did not want to listen to you, he would not ask for the details. There is an exception. The person who asks questions and doesn't wait for your answer is not truly interested. Questions of sincere interest are followed by a pause of sufficient length to permit you to answer. These sincere questions are sure signs of high receptivity and interest, and they give you your opportunity to talk.

Measure Your Impact

Finally, no matter how interesting you think you are, only the other person really knows. The only way you can find out is to ask. However, you can't very well ask, "Am I interesting?" Measure your impact by asking about your topic. If you are talking about music, ask, "What do you think of this type of music?" If you are talking about travel, ask, "Do you like to travel?" or "What do you think of this method of travel?" The answers to those questions will tell you whether or not your conversation was interesting.

HOW TO TURN QUOTATIONS INTO
CONVERSATIONAL MAGIC

There are two important ways to use quotations to develop conversational magic. One is to memorize quotations that will help you in conversation by providing helpful hints; the other is to reword quotations to add flavor and interest to your speech.

Memorize "Helpful Hint" Quotations

Most people enjoy colorful phrases that contain a message. They enjoy the helpfulness of the message and are stimulated by the colorful phrase or quotation that is used to deliver the message or helpful hint. Even people who reject direct advice respond to quotations. They can accept the hint from a quotation as though it were a universal truth rather than personal advice. A quotation carries the power of having survived through a period of time and having been tested by time.

A most famous quotation gives a helpful hint from Rudyard Kipling.

> I keep six honest serving men
> (They taught me all I knew);
> Their names are What and Why and When
> And How and Where and Who.

Another even more famous, the words of Robert Burns:

> Oh wad some power the giftie gie us
> To see oursel's as others see us!

These quotations are deceivingly simple in that they point to the value of gaining information on the first level and may be taken in that light. On a deeper examination, however, the real power of these quotations becomes evident. The six questions referred to by Kipling provide the critical examination of a situation that results in a thorough understanding of the details and concepts of the situation, the insight of drawing those details into a philosophical whole, and the power of controlling the conversation and the situation.

Burns' deeper meaning, though clearer in context, is just as powerful. The possibility of personality development shows clearly at the deeper level. If we see ourselves as others see us, we see our personality impairments and correct them. We see the strengths in our personality and use them to our best advantage.

By memorizing five or six quotations such as those of Kipling and Burns, you not only develop conversational magic, but also gain a valuable technique for improving your own personality. The rewards are a more pleasant, interesting, exciting, and popular you.

Reword Quotations to Add Flavor and Interest to Your Speech

Another way to add interest to your conversation is to reword quotations that are out of date. Select a quotation that contains an insightful or powerful message and reword it in modern terms that captures the essence of the original quotation.

For example, change the quote from Horace into a more explicit and modern metaphor or paraphrase. Horace said,

> The more a man denies himself,
> the more shall he obtain from God.

This thought might be paraphrased to read, "The more humble a man remains in thought, the more perceptive he becomes." Another paraphrase might be, "He who turns from material pursuits gains more than material gains can ever match." With a little thought you can take any quotation or metaphor and paraphrase it to express the same or a similar message. These paraphrases will enhance your image and improve the quality of your conversation.

HOW JOHN BOOKER USES QUOTATIONS TO PUT MAGIC INTO HIS CONVERSATION

John Booker, a recent college graduate when he joined our toastmasters' club two years ago, had great difficulty when trying to talk to people in groups. During an evaluation session after John had given a speech, his evaluator told John that he was improving; he was sure John would make further progress in the future. John responded with, "Walt Whitman says, 'The future is not more uncertain than the present.'" To hear John react so spontaneously with a quotation caught the imagination of the club members.

They encouraged John to use quotes in his speeches and conversations. John found this an excellent technique to involve himself in conversation. He rapidly overcame his speaking difficulty by using a quote to summarize or clarify what other people were saying. He was nicknamed "Quick Quote John" and provided our club with many fine speeches and enjoyable quotes. He overcame his problem in speaking with groups by developing his ability, to use quotations, into conversational magic.

HOW TO PUT FROSTING ON THE CONVERSATIONAL CAKE

To put the frosting on the conversational cake, you must have a good disposition, be positive in conversation, and avoid the inconsiderate remarks and actions that might irritate the people you talk to.

Improving Your Own Disposition

First of all, remember to be yourself. There is no value in pretending to be something you are not. If for example, you pretend to agree with a political, economic or social policy that you really don't believe in, you will eventually lose the respect of your friends. No one wants agreement at the cost of honesty. The trick is to keep your position but do so in a polite and friendly way.

Listen for Understanding. Listen carefully to what other people say. Most arguments result not from two different points of view but rather from a misunderstanding of two slightly different approaches to a problem. To improve your own disposition and make a better presentation of your own point of view, listen carefully to what the other person says. Make sure you understand the similarities between your own and the other person's position. Many people miss these similarities by looking for differences.

Speak for Understanding. When speaking, keep emotion out of your presentation. Don't let uncontrolled emotion cause you to criticize, yell at, or belittle your verbal opponent. People react negatively to what they consider uncontrolled emotion or unreasonable criticism. You will do much better in making your point if you speak clearly, pause for understanding, and answer all questions patiently and honestly. The better understanding people have of what you say, the more likely they are to agree with your point of view.

Be Positive in Conversation

No one wants to constantly hear negative comments. Negativism has a tendency to create despair. If people are constantly bombarded with negative statements, they lose the will to strive for improvement. Of more immediate consequence to an individual trying to improve his conversational ability is the fact that people generally turn away from negative people. Your best approach is to always be positive. You can develop a positive attitude by using the following techniques.

1. Analyze negative thoughts.
2. Dispose of resentment, jealousy and fear.
3. Practice goodwill toward all people.

Analyze negative thoughts. If you feel negative about some plan or future event, analyze your negative thoughts and decide why you have these expectations. Think back to the first negative thought. What caused it? What happened that made you think you would fail? Does failure logically follow? Did you misread the facts? If the facts do present the likelihood of failure, then ask how you can overcome the negative factors and be successful.

Once you are aware of the changes that need to be made to make your plans successful, you can be positive by talking about those changes. You simply say things in a positive way based upon the changes and specify what those changes are.

Dispose of resentment, jealousy, and fear. You will find it easy to be positive in conversation if you cast aside resentment, jealousy and fear. By getting these negative feelings out of the way, you will naturally speak in positive phrases when talking about others. In the long run resentment, jealousy and fear only hurt you. Resentment and jealousy interfere with your thought processes and keep you from thinking creatively and productively. Be happy for the good fortune of others and express this happiness whenever you hear of someone's achievements.

Fear also causes undue concentration on negative thoughts. All fears should be analyzed to determine how serious the feared event is. Ask the following questions.

1. Is my fear valid?
2. How will it affect me if it occurs?
3. What can I do to avoid its occurence?
4. How can I lessen its impact if it does occur?
5. What is the very worst effect it can have on me?
6. How can I recover from its effect?
7. What good will it do to worry?
8. What are the chances it won't occur?
9. Who can help me?
10. How long will it take to recover from its effects?

Practice goodwill toward all people. Another way to improve your own disposition is to practice goodwill toward all people. Psychologists have shown that people who treat others with consideration, develop a feeling of friendliness towards others. As they act with courtesy or kindness, their efforts are rewarded by a return of kindness and goodwill. You can improve your own disposition and reap rewards by practicing friendliness and goodwill toward all people.

Avoid Inconsiderate Remarks and Actions

The most usual reason that people fail to achieve the goals they train for, prepare for, and work for is that they develop personality problems. They knowingly or unknowingly develop habitual inconsiderate remarks and actions. This egotistical degrading of others eventually results in adverse reaction and rejection by those influential people whom your success and achievement depends upon.

Good judgment, based upon reflection of your interactions with and reactions by people in daily conversations, will determine the remarks and actions that may interfere with your success. The following list of verbal and non-verbal behavior was found to be offensive to people. People who responded to the questionnaire indicated a reaction ranging from "Slightly Disturbed" to "Intensely Angered."

Not listening to me	Gimmicky
Interrupting me	Exploits
Ignoring me	Bends Facts
High pressuring me	Defensive
Overcontrolling	Rambles
Sarcastic	Smoothes over
Demeaning	Vague
Blames others	Apathetic
Hostile	Coughing in my face
Selfish	Cheating
Manipulates	Smelling dirty
Bulldozes	Unfair
Moody	Harsh treatment of adults
Pouts	Harsh treatment of children
Withdraws	Blowing smoke in my face

JANET LALUCCI'S MAGIC CHARM IN CONVERSATION

Janet Lalucci is a natural conversationalist. She is charming, polite and considerate of other people. Janet had once been aggressive and hostile toward other people. Being intelligent and ambitious, she had worked diligently to gain promotion. Once in a supervisory position, Janet's ego came into play. She did a lot of talking and less and less listening to her subordinates. She used high pressure tactics, made demeaning remarks, and treated her subordinates as inferior people.

Productivity started to drop in Janet's department—each week it became lower. Her orders, demands, and high pressure tactics failed. In desperation she went to her boss, who was by then well aware of the problem. Her boss suggested a behavioral management seminar. Janet attended the seminar and during a personality assessment session learned how her behavior was affecting her subordinates.

At the seminar, Janet developed a set of personality improvement goals, which eventually led to her current pleasing personality. Janet began to treat her subordinates with dignity and respect. She listened carefully to what they had to say and in so doing gained new respect for them. Soon productivity was back to normal. The employees forgot Janet's treatment of them prior to attending the management seminar. Janet had changed and so had the employees. She learned to respect them, and they learned to respect and work productively for her.

6

How Conversational Magic Can Help You Understand and Deal with Other People

The major problem we have in dealing with people is one of understanding. We don't understand the backgrounds and motivations of people and consequently can't predict their individual reactions to the things we say and do. If we can gain some insight into other people's backgrounds and their motivations, we can deal with them more effectively.

This chapter concentrates on conversational techniques that evoke information from the people you talk to. You'll learn to develop the information you need to better understand other people and to use that understanding to deal with them on a more productive and friendly basis.

You'll see examples, of people using conversational techniques to gain understanding and deal more effectively with people in all situations. You can use these same techniques in your daily interactions with friends and co-workers. By learning to understand people better, you also learn to deal with them more effectively in achieving your personal and business goals.

ADDING CONVERSATIONAL MAGIC
TO THE PHILOSOPHY OF "DO UNTO OTHERS"

The philosophy of doing unto others as you would have them do unto you applies in conversation as well as in physical behavior. In other words, "Speak as courteously and considerately to others as you would have them speak to you. Harsh, aggressive, or inconsiderate language should not be used in conversation. The magic in this courteous approach is that it gains the other person's respect for you.

The Home-Spun Philosopher

My friend Mort says that the "Do unto others" doctrine should be amended to say, "Do unto others as they would like to be done to." Sometimes, Mort believes, what we like for ourselves is not appropriate for the other person. Each of us is different, and as we learn to understand one another better we begin to understand that we often prefer to be treated differently.

Mort illustrates his philosophy by telling a story about his friend "Kerosene" Joe. Joe believes that kerosene will cure anything. For example, when Joe gets the "flu," he takes two teaspoons of kerosene every four hours. Joe swears it cured his cough and fever. Mort says Joe suffered side effects from the kerosene. Joe lost his voice, has a nervous twitch, and has suffered two heart attacks. He just doesn't believe the kerosene caused it though. Mort says that no one has ever seen Joe take the kerosene, but he believes Joe because of the side effects.

It's obvious that Joe can't go around doing unto others as he would do unto himself. He would soon be charged with murder. The same principle applies in conversation. If we want to wield that old conversational magic and increase our popularity and success with people, we must first understand what they like and want. Then treat them and talk to them in terms of their own personal likes and desires.

Understanding Through Questioning

The most effective way of gaining understanding of other people is through asking questions. There are three basic types of information-gaining questions.

1. Questions that evoke feelings.
2. Questions that seek opinions.
3. Questions that require evaluation.

Questions that evoke feelings. You may ask for people's feelings simply by saying, "How do you feel about . . .?" or "What are your feelings on . . .?" use any topic of interest or current concern. If for example, you are interested in a current political problem, ask the other person how he feels about that problem. The answer will give you some understanding of him.

If you ask about dealing with a foreign country and the other person immediately responds with a comment that the foreign country should be bombed or "wiped off the face of the earth," the responding person is of course revealing his or her basic feelings about how to solve problems. One comment or one question, however, will not provide a full understanding of a person's feelings and attitudes because there may be a special element involved in the situation. If a person's family was killed by the foreign country, he or she may be hostile toward that country without holding the same hostile feelings toward others.

You can test your understanding, however, by asking additional questions about other national, state or local problems. The feelings expressed in each of the situations will begin to form a pattern. The expressed feelings will either tend to be hostile and aggressive or they will tend to be warm and understanding. If the answers seem to be neutral rather than hostile or warm, the other person may not understand the issue. If after discussion, the responses are still neutral, again you have a better understanding of the person you are dealing with.

The same pattern of feelings will carry over into all aspects of life. If the pattern is one of hostility, you will understand that the person your are talking to is generally going to take a hostile approach in dealing with people. If you do not wish to become involved with someone with such hostile feelings, you are free to get away from him before a friendship develops that you may later regret.

Questions that seek opinions. The same questioning techniques used to gather feelings can also evoke opinions. They are often expressed when not asked for, but you can ask, "What is your view of . . . ?" or, "Would you mind giving me your opinion on this situation?" Then explain the situation.

The opinions another expresses will give you insight into the make-up of that person. The more opinions you hear him express, the better you will understand him. Our opinions reflect our background, assumptions and beliefs, which are the framework from which we form opinions about any specific problem or situation.

By listening carefully to the opinions people express, you can gain a better understanding of them. Think about what they are saying and ask yourself the question, "Is that a hostile or warm attitude?" By thinking about the comments and answers to your questions, you can learn people's personality characteristics much more rapidly than you normally could. Many people ignore clues that hostile people give and form close friendships with these hostile people. They are later surprised when their new friends express this hostility in situations that are embarrassing or harmful.

Questions that require evaluation. The third type of question to be used to gain understanding is to ask for an evaluation. The evaluation the other person makes reflects his or her own personality traits. So, you can evaluate the personality of the person giving the response as he evaluates the situation you described.

The easy part of this type of questioning is that you can draw upon events that have already occurred for the question. You can ask the other person to compare recent court decisions. Or, you can ask for an evaluation of the president's or some other political figure's current decisions.

You can pick any topic, ranging from sports to philosophy, from the first recorded history to current events, and select any situation of interest for an evaluation. The way the other person evaluates the event, the consequences, the decision, or the actions of the people involved reveals his or her own inner personality traits. By listening, questioning and evaluating you can understand people better and deal with them more effectively.

How George Anthony's Understanding of Other People Changed His Life

George Anthony believed the world to be a "Dog eat dog" place to live. His past experience with hostile people had convinced him that all people were out to take advantage of each other. George consequently developed a hostile attitude toward the world. This resulted in hostile behavior on the job and kept George in trouble there.

George's hostile behavior slowly became habitual and pervaded all of his social and business relationships including his relationship with his family. Soon his family and friends were unhappy and resented George's behavior toward them. Just short of a divorce, George agreed to family counseling and that counseling became the turning point in George's life. For the first time George became aware that everyone is not hostile.

Once George learned that not all people are hostile, he was susceptible to ideas about the different drives that affect behavior. He learned that people are different, have different goals, and more importantly need to be treated differently.

Slowly George began to change. He began to consider the needs of his family and friends. He found that he could consider their needs without any major loss of his own. As a matter of simple appreciation, his family and friends became more considerate of him. George saw the results of the different way he was treating his friends and decided to try to learn more about the people he worked with.

George began to use the three questioning techniques to get a better understanding of the people he worked with. Slowly he gained an understanding of his co-workers and began to treat them with more understanding and courtesy. People soon forgot how hostile George had been in the past, and he became one of the most well-liked and popular people in the office.

HOW UNDERSTANDING OTHER PEOPLE HELPS YOU IN CONVERSATION

Psychologists and other researchers have divided people into various personality classifications. These personality types can be studied in relation to how the person will react to conversational tactics. For example, some people become fearful and withdraw if too many questions or questions that seem personal are asked. Others become irritated when one person talks too much and doesn't pause and give them an opportunity to respond.

Personality profiles have been drawn and labeled type "A" and "B," or labeled with names such as the "Driver" and "Supporter," The classification I like is one that names the reactive or proactive behavior of the personality style. Thus, just by stating the name, you describe the behavior you have to deal with.

These four classifications: Destructive, Defensive, Disruptive and Diagnostic will cover almost any behavior you encounter. Therefore, by learning and understanding them, you will be able to deal with any personality type.

How to Use Conversational Magic to Deal with the Destructive Personality

One objective of the Destructive personality is to develop power over other people. The Destructive personality tries to achieve this in conversation by dominating and controlling the conversation. Recent university studies have shown that males generally establish power over females by three simple techniques: (1) interrupting the female, (2) not responding to topics introduced by the female, and (3) dominating the conversation by bringing up personal topics of interest.

In cases where the female interrupted more often than the male did, the research study found clear evidence that the female was the more powerful and dominant member in the relationship. The study clearly established interrupting as a method of exercising power by violating the other person's right to speak.

Even on first meeting, people were found to interrupt, fail to respond, and introduce topics of personal interest as a method of establishing dominance. These techniques are typical of the Destructive personality as this person tries to establish power in conversation.

A natural and easy way to deal with the Destructive personality is to ask questions. This is easy for men and already a habit for most women. Many studies have shown that women are more courteous in conversation than men. They habitually ask questions about the topic brought up by the other person.

When a question is asked, the Destructive personality is given a chance to fulfill the underlying need for respect and esteem, the driving force underlying the desire for power. The question then short-circuits the power move by saying, in effect, "I respect your feelings and opinions. You don't have to make a power play to earn my respect."

When dealing, in conversation, with the Destructive personality, you simply short-circuit this person's destructive actions. You ask questions, you respond to his topics of interest and act courteously at all times. Do not let the Destructive personality push you around either physically or verbally. Stand your ground in a firm but polite way. Do not pretend agreement when you don't. Simply say, "I respect your opinion, but I don't share your viewpoint."

Finally, the Destructive personality is very difficult to deal with. As soon as you find that someone you know is most often performing as the Destructive personality type, you must decide whether or not he is worth knowing at all. The reason I say "most often" is that usually people don't display this Destructive personality all the time. Some display it all the time, but others only display it when irritated. The clue might be how easily is that person irritated.

In those situations where you are trapped with a Destructive personality, be polite but assertive. When interrupted, simply say, "Pardon me, I'm not finished," or "May I just finish this thought?" If you are interrupted again, just say, "I'm still not finished," or "I'll be finished in just a second." By standing up for your rights in a polite way, you will win the respect of the Destructive personality and have fewer problems with him.

How to Use Conversational Magic to Deal with the Defensive Personality

The Defensive personality is operating from a base of fear. Fear that he may say the wrong thing and look stupid or be ridiculed. Because of this fear, the Defensive personality becomes embarrassed easily. One reason for his defensiveness is this fear of embarrassment, so one reinforces the other.

The Defensive personality is generally quiet. He seldom starts a conversation and responds very little in conversation. When asked questions, he generally keeps his answers as short as possible. He feels the less he says, the less chance there is for trouble.

There is usually an underlying hostility that may not be suspected in the Defensive personality. Just because this person is on the defensive, however, doesn't mean that he likes it. He simply doesn't feel as powerful as other people. He thinks he would lose in open conflict. He, therefore, builds up hostility which is often expressed in subtle sarcasm or sarcastic jokes.

The Defensive person is always alert, on the defense, trusting no one, waiting for the worst to happen. If you do or say anything to embarass, degrade, or in any way put down the Defensive personality, you prove to him that his suspicions about you were right. And the Defensive personality is always suspicious of everyone.

The way to deal with the Defensive personality, should you want or be forced to, is to keep in mind his suspicions and defensive nature and never do anything that confirms his suspicion or pressures him in any way.

With that guideline in mind, you can lead a Defensive person in conversation. First ask questions that require more than just a "yes" or "no" answer. Also the three question types explained earlier in this chapter. For example, ask, "How do you feel about . . .?", "What do you think of . . .?", "What is your opinion of . . .?" or, "How would you evaluate, compare, contrast . . .?"

These questions require some explanation and will get the Defensive person to talk. Once he begins to talk, listen carefully, pay attention to what he says, and make some comments to show that you listened and understand his point. If you don't understand, ask for a clarification. That too shows that you were listening. Remember, the Defensive personality is suspicious. He thinks you won't really listen to him.

How to Use Conversational Magic to Deal with the Disruptive Personality

The Disruptive personality is not necessarily hostile. In fact, most people who disrupt conversations or meetings do so from a fun-loving attitude or from a desire to be friendly. The problem is that they don't know when to stop. They let the tricks and gags get out of hand, or they continue to talk about irrelavant issues which interfere with productive discussion.

The underlying motivation for the Disruptive personality is one of warmth and friendliness. This person wants to be liked, wants to be popular, wants to be successful, but in overdoing his friendly act, he fails to accomplish his objective. By talking too much, by not listening enough, and by denying the other person equal time, the Disruptive personality actually irritates and turns the very people against him whose friendship he is trying to win.

To deal effectively with the Disruptive personality, you must continually draw him back to the important topic of general interest or the topic you wish discussed. Since the Disruptive personality likes to talk, keep him talking about your topic of interest.

Bring him back to the main topic by using directed questions and comments. Directed questions are those that pertain to and require an answer related to the main topic of discussion. For example, if the main topic is politics, keep drawing the Disruptive personality back to politics by asking for his opinion, feelings, or evaluation of some political event.

Directed comments are those that direct the conversation by a statement that leads to further comment or controversy. By making a comment such as "I feel politics is a very worthy endeavor," you evoke either a similar comment or an opposing viewpoint. Those directed comments and questions can be used continually until you are satisfied that the interest in the main topic has been satisfied.

How to Use Conversational Magic to Deal with the Diagnostic Personality

The Diagnostic personality usually looks for logic, reason, and truth. This person is analytical in thought and is generally a good problem solver. He or she leans heavily on facts, figures, and other forms of evidence. As a general rule, evidence is the key element the Diagnostic personality dwells on. This person looks for and then bases his or her actions upon the evidence found.

The Diagnostic personality seems warm and friendly because he or she generally is a good listener. Always seeking information, this person listens to ideas, opinions, facts, figures or any information you are willing to share. The Diagnostic type, due to his patience and willingness to listen, usually gains a true respect and develops a warm appreciation for people. A few, unfortunately, hold a hostile view toward all people and try to manipulate them for their own ends.

To deal with the Diagnostic personality, simply be honest and candid. If you chose not to reveal certain information that this person asks for, don't beat around the bush or try to mislead. The Diagnostic personality will see right through any attempt at deception. This personality type will respect a candid refusal to reveal personal information. So, either answer truthfully, or candidly explain your reason for not answering.

Your participation in conversation with the Diagnostic type person need not be submissive and hesitant. You can participate fully by asking questions. This is an excellent opportunity to learn. The Diagnostic personality is loaded with detailed information and is usually willing and anxious to share it.

You can win friendship and popularity when dealing with the Diagnostic personality type by both supplying and seeking information. This person appreciates information and responds to people who supply it. They also respond favorably to people who ask questions because they can fulfill their own ego needs by showing how much they know by answering questions.

How Wilma Abbot Used
Her Understanding of Other People
to Become a Popular Conversationalist

Wilma Abbot was a quiet, lonely lady who was unable to talk to people. If she acted friendly, it never seemed to work. Either the other person seemed hostile or she couldn't think of anything to keep the conversation going. Eventually, Wilma learned about the four personality types and things began to change.

Wilma studied and responded appropriately to each of the four personality types. With the Destructive personality, she learned to ask questions and listen, let him express his hostility, and yet retain her own assertiveness. With the Defensive personality, she learned to be considerate, polite and avoid any pressure. She gives the Defensive person ample time to formulate his or her thoughts and listens patiently while they are being expressed.

She learned to lead and guide the Disruptive personality by making statements or asking questions that keep him on the track. She learned to deal with the Diagnostic personality by responding openly with the information he wanted, and by asking for information that permits the Diagnostic personality to express his or her knowledge. Nancy overcame her shyness and her loneliness. She became more and more popular as she learned more about other people.

7

How to Use Listening Skills to Improve Your Conversation

You have probably given a lot of thought to developing your conversational expertise, but how much thought have you given to listening? Everyone is concerned with speaking well and making interesting conversation, yet most of us forget that listening is the most important component of conversation. There are two very important reasons for listening. One is to determine what the other person's point of view is; the second is to determine whether or not the other person understands your point of view.

In this chapter you'll see how to improve your conversation by using better listening techniques. Listening techniques that leave a positive impression, build personal benefits and improve your conversational ability are all covered in this chapter. By using them, you will become a more popular conversationalist.

FOUR WAYS THAT LISTENING IMPROVES YOUR CONVERSATION

There is no doubt that listening improves our conversation. Most of us intend to listen, but often fail to do so because of poor habits that have been carried over from childhood. To determine whether or not you need to improve your listening habits, ask yourself the following questions:

1. Do I show interest by nodding or making brief comments?
2. Do I interrupt before the speaker completes his or her thoughts?
3. Do I listen for major facts?
4. Do I try to remember key points?
5. Do I listen "between the lines" for second meanings?
6. Am I easily distracted when listening?
7. Do I develop mental arguments against the points the speaker makes?
8. Do I try to understand why the speaker's opinion differs from my own?
9. Do I hold my emotions in check while listening?
10. Do I check my understanding with the speaker before expressing an opposing opinion?

Answers to questions number 2, 6 and 7 should be no. All other questions should be answered yes. If your answers differ from the ones given here, then you have been honest in answering and can work on correcting those that are different. The four following explanations of how listening improves your conversation will provide the logic for improving your listening habits.

Uncovering Topics That Interest Other People

Listening uncovers topics that interest other people. People reveal their interests by the way they talk. A person who is interested in sports, for example, will talk about sports. Not only will this person reveal his interest by directly discussing sports, he will also use sports for comparison with other topics and is likely to joke about sports.

By listening between the lines, for example, you can determine a speaker's area of interest. If the speaker is talking about economics but uses comparisons to sports or tells jokes from a sports orientation to make his or her point, you may assume that the speaker is strongly interested in sports.

An optician reported learning a lot about his patients by listening to their jokes. One man whom he asked to read the fourth line, responded with "C H W R K." The patient added, "I can read it but I can't pronounce it. I believe it is a pitcher for the Dodgers." The optician correctly surmized that the man's joke indicated an interest in baseball. A few questions revealed him to be an avid baseball fan.

By listening carefully for the extraneous remarks, jokes, comments, and questions, you will gain an understanding of the things that interest that person. Then you can improve your own conversation by commenting on or asking questions about those known areas of interest.

Preventing Unfounded Regrettable Statements

One of the defective aspects in interrupting a speaker before that person has completed his or her thought, is that your statement may reflect an incorrect assumption about the speaker's intended remark. Not only is your statement unfounded, but you have also accused your friend or acquaintance of saying something that was never said. Nothing can be more unfair than to accuse a speaker of saying something that you misunderstood as a result of your incorrect assumption.

You can avoid regrettable statements that infer the other speaker has made a disagreeable remark by being determined never to interrupt anyone. You can always check to be sure simply by asking the other person "Have you completed your comment?" If not, the other person will say so and continue to speak. If the person has finished, he or she will then listen to you.

If you interrupt someone before he finishs his thought, he will be distracted by the desire to finish his comments and will not listen anyway. There's an old story about an English parlimentarian who was being interrupted from the floor. The parlimentarian, anxious to end the interruption, tried to embarrass the hecklers. He raised his voice and said, "There seems to be a number of fools here tonight who wish to argue. I wonder if we could hear one at a time?" "Aye," came the reply, "Finish your speech."

This turn of events shows the fallacy in trying to insult someone who interrupts you. The way to handle interruptions is to simply say to the person, "Excuse me, I wasn't finished." Then continue with your comments. Each time you are interrupted, very politely repeat that you were not finished and continue your comments.

Determining Bias or Unsupported Claims

Another value of listening is that you can determine bias or recognize claims that may not be true because they are unsupported. By being aware and listening for unsupported claims, you will be less likely to be mislead in conversation.

Listen for half-truths. The speaker may select only favorable information and withhold the unfavorable information, or may present facts that seem true but only really do half of what they are supposed to do. Sometimes the speaker will use facts that support a similar but not the same idea he is supporting. He then implies that he has proven his point. All of these unethical methods can be guarded against by listening carefully and analyzing the information presented.

Establishing Conversational Rapport

Listening not only gains information and understanding, it develops conversational rapport. If you listen attentively, you develop a friendly atmosphere in which the other person is willing to listen to you. The fact that you are courteous, listen attentively, and really try to understand the other person's point of view develops a conversational rapport. He then reacts the same way—he becomes courteous, listens attentively, and really tries to understand your point of view.

You can develop this conversational rapport by applying the following listening steps.

1. *Listen attentively.* Nod your head and comment with "Uh huh," or "I see."
2. *Be neutral.* Do not criticize or disagree with the other person.
3. *Ask for clarification.* Ask questions to clear up any point you don't fully understand.
4. *Summarize main points.* Restate the other person's main points before you comment on them. Make sure that he agrees to your interpreting him.

5. *Present your point and pause.* When your present your point of view, make one point and then pause so that the other person can absorb what you've said and respond if he so desires.

How Jim Used Listening Techniques with His Children

Jim Wellington, an auto salesman, had recently increased his sales after learning to use listening techniques with his auto customers. He was so successful, in fact, that he began to really appreciate the value of listening.

Jim had never been very successful in getting his children to understand his point of view and respond the way he wanted them to. Since he was unable to achieve his goals by telling his children what to do, Jim decided that he would try the listening techniques that had been so successful at work.

Jim used the five steps that establish conversational rapport. When talking to one of his children, first he listened attentively to his child's point of view. He remained neutral, did not cirticize or disagree with what was said. He seriously tried to understand the child's viewpoint. If there was any point he disagreed with or did not fully understand, he asked the child for clarification.

Then, before Jim made any comments expressing his own point of view, he summarized the child's main points. In other words, he showed the child that he really did understand. He might not agree but he did understand the child's opinion. At this point, Jim would present his own viewpoint. He would express his opinion and tell his child what he would like done.

Not surprisingly, the children began to listen more carefully and clarify their own thoughts and opinions. Then more often than not, they accepted the view of the parent who was interested enough to take the time to understand them.

THE BENEFITS OF LISTENING

Listening is a beneficial activity. Many jokes have been developed that show the value of listening. One is the saying, "God gave us one mouth and two ears. That doesn't seem to indicate he wanted us to talk twice as much as we listen!" Another is the comment made by a worker coming out of his boss' office.

He said, "I just had a long talk with the boss. Well really, I guess he had the long talk; I had a long listen."

How Listening Builds Respect

Listening to another is a sign that you value his opinion. Listening without interrupting shows that you are too interested in what he is saying to cut him off. Trying to get a clear understanding of what the other person means indicates respect and appreciation for what that person has to say. Now think how you would feel if someone you were talking to did those three things. Wouldn't you respect that person? That's how listening builds respect. By showing respect, you build respect for yourself.

How Listening Helps the Speaker

Primary research done by Dr. Carl Rogers revealed that a person who is listened to attentively will begin to think about what he is saying. As he thinks, he begins to clarify his own thoughts. When the speaker sees that you are really interested, as when you ask questions, he begins to think more logically in order to more clearly answer your questions. So we see that listening helps the speaker think more clearly and express himself more logically.

How Listening Helps the Listener

Listening helps you, the listener, develop a clear understanding of the speaker's viewpoint, and also helps you determine what impression you have previously made on the other person. By listening carefully to his response, you can determine how much impact your previous remarks had on him. There are numerous effects that your conversation may have on the other person. You may cause him to become frustrated and angry, or you may capture his interest and imagination. If he becomes frustrated and angry you have made a negative impact and he will not listen to you. Noticing this, you may change your approach and develop a better rapport for future conversations.

How Marty Sills Used Listening to Get a Promotion

Marty Sills, who was a very aggressive person, worked hard and got good results. He eventually noticed that his peers were promoted, but he was stuck on the same job. Though Marty changed departments, the same thing happened again. Finally, Marty asked his supervisor why he was being passed. The supervisor replied that Marty was held back because he didn't listen.

Marty argued about his good performance to no avail. He had to face the fact that, in spite of his good performance, he would not be promoted until he learned to listen. This was a slow and painful process because Marty really preferred to talk. Slowly, however, he learned to withhold his comments until the other person had spoken. As he learned to listen to his superiors, he was surprised to find that their ideas worked, also. Marty became a good listener and finally received his promotion.

LISTENING TECHNIQUES
THAT LEAVE POSITIVE IMPRESSIONS

By learning and using the techniques covered in this section, you can walk away from any person or group knowing that you have left a positive impression. These methods will show the other person or group of people that you are an intelligent, poised, considerate, and interesting person. You will reveal your underlying values and leave a good impression in all situations. All you have to do is learn and use these four listening techniques.

Listen Analytically and
Don't Jump to Conclusions

A basic problem with people who don't listen analytically is that they jump to conclusions. They hear only a phrase or sentence, often out of context, and jump to a conclusion. This often results in an argument which leaves a poor impression. Even if you win the argument, you still leave a negative impression.

By listening analytically, by really trying to understand the other person's point of view, and by asking questions when you don't agree with the other person, you will often find your differences disappear. Even if the differences remain, if you take this analytical approach, you will understand the other person's position and be less likely to argue or dispute his word. When the discussion has ended, you may not have changed his opinion. On the other hand, how many opinions have you changed with argument? One thing you will do, by listening analytically, is leave a positive impression.

Ask Questions Without Mental Argument

Many people ask questions in such a way that they antagonize the person they ask. Some people can ask questions all day and never irritate or antagonize the other person. In many cases the reason for the different results is the attitude expressed. The Antagonistic questioner reveals his hidden mental argument in the way he asks his questions. The words he chooses, his tone of voice, and the look on his face all reveal his argumentative mental state.

You can avoid this problem by refusing to let yourself become mentally argumentative. Be determined to listen with an open mind. Ask questions with a true desire to learn. Ask questions that will help you understand the other person's feelings and opinions. Ask, "Why do you feel this way?", or, "How did you reach this conclusion?" Any question that politely requests the information the other person used in developing his opinions is fair if it is not asked in a way that reflects an attitude of mental argument.

By practicing asking questions in a polite, considerate way, you will soon become very good at gathering the information you need. The following questioning techniques may be helpful.

1. *Ask easy questions.* Ask questions that do not require deep thought, mathematical computation or technical analysis.
2. *Ask informational questions.* Ask the so-called "W" questions—who, when, where, what, why and how.
3. *Ask hypothetical questions.* Ask questions that begin with, "Suppose," "Imagine," or "What if." These questions are helpful to the person who has a problem making decisions. Hypothetical questions often help the other person think and see his problem more clearly.
4. *Ask explanatory questions.* Ask for explanations, examples, or evidence to support the other person's feelings or point of view.

Limit Your Own Talking and Never Interrupt

A psychologist friend of mine tells of a time he almost interrupted a patient but held his mouth in check; the patient soon clarified his thoughts without having been interrupted. The psychologist said to the patient, "Why don't you start at the beginning and tell me everything about yourself." The patient said, "O.K. In the beginning I created the heavens and the earth." At this point the psychologist was tempted to interrupt but did not. The patient soon clarified that there is a little of God in all of us, and the good we do is an extension of God's beginning.

Interrupting is never acceptable. When we interrupt, we say, "Your information is not worth listening to, but mine is, so listen to me and don't interrupt me." By establishing a goal to limit your own talking, you will be less likely to interrupt. For example, you might set your goal so that you strive to speak only one sentence for every three the other person speaks.

If you have a problem frequently interrupting others, you may always ask if the other person is through before speaking. Another technique is to summarize the other person's previous statements before you speak. These techniques will leave a positive impression and enhance your reputation.

Evaluate the Evidence Without Emotional Reaction by Programming Your Listening

A good listener evaluates evidence without emotional reaction. One way to divorce yourself from emotionalism is to program your listening and weigh both points of view.

A good listening program separates fact from emotion. By planning a program of fact finding, you draw your own attention to facts and away from emotional appeal. The following five points will keep you on the facts.

1. *Prepare in advance.* Find out something about the people or person to whom you are going to talk. Set your mind to learn something from that person.
2. *Listen for central or main ideas.* By determining the main theme or central idea the other person is pre-

senting, you will be able to recognize the emotional appeals and separate them from the evidence that really supports the main idea.

3. *Relate subordinate points to the central or main idea.* As you listen to each bit of evidence or subordinate point, think how those points relate to the main idea. When you carefully evaluate the points, you may see that some do not really support the main idea.

4. *Listen for illogical conclusions.* Often unscrupulous speakers will try to win your support or change your opinion by drawing illogical conclusions. If, after stating a number of points of evidence, a speaker draws a conclusion that doesn't seem to follow, think back over the points made and determine whether or not his conclusion is logical.

5. *Weigh both points of view.* Quite often we find ourselves listening to a person who holds an opposing viewpoint. We think we can change another's opinion if we can get him to listen to our view. As discussed earlier, if we wish to get someone to listen to us, we must also listen to him. We should listen to the other person open-mindedly. We should try to understand his logic, examine his evidence and weigh his conclusions against the evidence presented. Then we can present our point of view in relation to the evidence he has presented. Some of our facts may agree with his, some may not. We should accept those we agree with and point out those that we do not agree with. Next, we point out the areas of disagreement. Present the points of disagreement one at a time and ask for a reaction to our evidence. One at a time, point by point, the areas of disagreement can be resolved. If we each present our evidence, let the other respond to it and examine our reasons for disagreement, this two-way method of communications will resolve most arguments.

How Mary James Used Listening Techniques to Improve Her Conversation

Mary James became aware that she often jumped to conclusions before people finished talking, when her small son asked, "Where did I come from?" Mary related the general concepts of conception, growth, and birth to the son who acted genuinely interested. When she concluded however, the son asked "But I mean, what state did I come from? All the other kids know their state."

After the incident, Mary began to make certain she understood the question she was asked before forming a conclusion and giving an answer. No matter how interesting or intelligent the wrong answer, it's still the wrong answer.

As Mary listened more carefully and asked questions for clarification, she began to understand other people better, relate better to their ideas and opinions, and speak more intelligently and respectfully to others. Her conversation improved, people liked and respected her more, and she began to enjoy conversation more.

8

How to Use "Conversational Timing" to Enhance Your Popularity

Popularity often hinges upon a few words, or more precisely upon how the few words are spoken. Sarcasm, patriotism, emotionalism, or inattention to others may result in a lack of popularity, but the most probable cause of a lack of popularity is poor timing. Trying to be funny, wise, dominant, debonaire or simply trying to make a serious point at the wrong time can result in a loss of popularity.

In this chapter, the conditions that create poor timing are explained. Clues that people give to indicate that they are not receptive and will respond negatively are identified so that you can tell when your timing is wrong. Then techniques are explained that will create better timing. Finally you'll see how to recognize the correct time and see how to make your point when the time is right.

CONVERSATIONAL CLUES THAT TELL YOU WHEN YOUR TIMING IS RIGHT OR WRONG

Although many people realize the importance of timing, most do not recognize the clues that people give to tell us when our timing is right or wrong. By learning these clues, you will be able to determine the right or wrong time to make a point. Your improved timing, then, will win the respect of your friends and improve your popularity.

Recognizing the "Wrong Time" Clues

A recently appointed operations manager walked into the plant for his first inspection. He saw some safety equipment being used improperly, walked over to the shop steward, and remarked that the procedure should be changed. "We've had enough changes for one day," snapped the steward. All the worker's eyes were on the steward and the new operations manager. The manager snapped back, "When I come into a plant, I run it *my* way. I want the change made." The shop steward waved his hand and all work stopped. He looked the new manager in the eye and said, "Go ahead, run it."

Obviously the manager had missed an important clue that the time was wrong to institute a change. He should have developed a more receptive relationship with the steward before making a change.

People give two types of clues when your timing is wrong. One is the verbalization of anger or frustration which reflects a low level of receptivity to your ideas or opinions. This verbalization may include profanity, cutting remarks, yelling or mild criticism. Whenever you encounter mild criticism, be aware that this is the wrong time to try to make a point.

The other type of clue given by people are statements verbalized in authoritarian or non-negotiable statements. Examples are encountered frequently in everyday life. These clues are remarks such as:

> "I want it done my way."
> "You are wrong."
> "I'll make the decisions."
> "My mind is made up."
> "I've tried it before."
> "It won't work here."
> "I'm not interested."

"Skip the details."
"Do it now."
"Do as you're told."
"Do as I say, not as I do."
"This is the way it's going to be"
"I don't care what you say."
"You're wasting time."
"Be quiet and listen."
"I'm not going to make any changes."
"It's this way or else."
"I won't look at anything else."
"I don't care about quality, just give me the price."

Whenever you hear any of these or similar verbal clues, you should recognize them as signals that your timing is wrong. (For a more detailed explanation, see my book, *How to Use Psychological Leverage to Double the Power of What You Say*, p. 54, Parker Publishing Co., 1978.)

A Sale That Was Lost Because of Wrong Timing

Carl Waverly walked into the office of John Mellon prepared to sell a load of auto replacement parts. John complained that the previous salesman had overstocked him twice and that he would never give that salesman an order again. Carl failed to recognize that John's complaint was a clue to a low level of receptivity and a "wrong time" to make a sales presentation.

Carl began his presentation and John muttered a few unintelligible comments under his breath. Carl should have stopped at this time and explored John's concerns. He continued his presentation, however, because he had consistently been successful with it in the past.

Carl was surprised when, at the end of his presentation, he failed to get the order. John mentioned that he was just too distraught to do any buying today. If Carl had been observant, he would have recognized this and would have saved his presentation for a better time. As it was, he lost the sale because of the wrong timing.

Conversational Techniques That
Create the Correct Time

When people are verbalizing anger or authoritarian or non-negotiable statements, their receptivity is low. They need to vent the anger or talk through to completion the ideas behind their remarks. The completion process and the ventilation process lower people's concern for their own needs, and their level of receptivity rises. Remember, they must verbalize their feelings in order for the right time to be created.

You can help the other person ventilate or relieve his frustration and anger. There are a number of questions that you can ask that will encourage the other person to talk out his frustration and, in the process, create the "right time" to present your own point of view.

For example, if a parent says to a teen-ager: "Darn it, your grades in school are bad," the teen-ager may say: "You seem to be upset about my grades." Now, he may pause and let the parent start venting the emotion, or he may use a combination of probes. After saying: "You seem to be upset about my grades," the teen-ager may add, "Which of my grades is bothering you?"

If he used only the reflective probe, which is an acceptable approach, he would allow some time for the parent's response and then continue probing. During the continual probing he would ask questions to determine the point that upset the parent.

He may find that the parent is upset because of one particular grade. Or it may be all the grades. It may be a misunderstanding. The parent may be comparing the teen-ager's grades with grades of another member of the family. He may think the grades were higher the previous month than they were. His real anger may center around the belief that he was told the grades were going to be higher. So he may be angry because he thinks the teen-ager gave him false information, not because of the grades received.

It is important to recognize that people often show concern over one thing, but the real problem is caused by something else. Before the problem can be discussed and resolved, we must know what that real concern is. Probing does that job for us. Probing gets inside the other person's mind. With probing you learn the real feelings and opinions and what really concerns the other person rather than what you may have guessed. Guesses are often wrong.

To finish the example about grades, let's relate to Mary and her mother as Mary practices her probing techniques. Mary will try to help her mother vent her anger, and at the same time, gain understanding about the situation that is disturbing her mother.

Mother: "Darn it, your grades are bad." (Low receptivity).

Mary: "You certainly are upset about my grades." (Reflective probe).

Mother: "You can bet on that! I've got enough problems without you kids bringing home poor grades from school." (More intense anger, lower level of receptivity).

Mary: "Did someone else bring home poor grades?" (Probe for information).

Mother: "Yes. Your brother Bill." (Anger starts to subside. Receptivity starts up).

Mary: "What grades did Bill get?" (Information).

Mother: "Bill got two 'D's'." (Level of receptivity slowly rising).

Mary: "I can understand your concern about Bill's grades." (reflective probe).

Mother: "Yes it causes me a lot of concern. I don't know if he can catch up." (Uncertainty).

Mary: "I hope he does catch up, so you won't have to worry. By the way mother, I only have one 'C' on my report card. Is it the 'C' that concerns you?"

Mother: "Well, I'm not concerned about one 'C,' but after your father see's Bill's report card, he'll be so mad, he'll yell about yours, too."

Mary: "So it's Father's reaction that concerns you."

Mother: "Yes, I don't know what he'll say." (Correct time)

Mary: "Do you think he will be less angry, if he looks at my report card first?"

Mother: "Yes, he might. Let's show him your report card first. You can discuss the problems you had, and perhaps if he gets an understanding of your problems, he will be

in a more receptive state of mind when he talks to
Bill."

Mary: "O.K., I'll be thinking over how to explain my problem
before he gets here."

If Mary uses the same questioning techniques in dealing
with her father that she used in dealing with her mother, she
will have no problem. In dealing with her mother, she recognized
that her mother's level of receptivity was low and her timing was
wrong. She began the process of creating the right time by using
questioning or probing techniques and by expressing concern for
her mother's feelings. By using questions to draw out her
mother's fears and getting her to ventilate her emotions, she
created the correct time to explain her point of view.

Toni Zarder's Magic Rise in Popularity

Toni, a new employee, was having a difficult time in making
friends with the older employees who seemed to be formed into
cliques. Toni was becoming discouraged and began to feel sorry
she had joined the company. One morning she was stopped at
the water fountain by a lady who "talked her ear off." Toni
listened patiently, glad for an opportunity to talk to someone.
She questioned the lady about the things that irritated her and
learned of the problems that bothered the other women as well.

This gave Toni an insight into how to deal with the cliques.
By relating to their problems, she was able to talk to any of them
about something that interested them all. One by one, she won
their respect and friendship, and her popularity rose rapidly
until she became the most popular person in the office.

HOW TO SAY IT RIGHT WHEN YOUR TIMING IS RIGHT

When your timing is right, either a serious or humorous approach may be acceptable, depending upon the situation. I have
a friend who used humor even in high level business encounters.
Once while making a sales presentation to a large chain buyer,
he used humor to overcome the customer's resistance to buying

pork sausage. The salesman said, "This sausage is certified by the F.B.I." "What?" asked the customer. "Sure," replied the salesman. "It's certified to disappear under heat." That time the customer laughed, but care should be used when dealing with humor. It might turn the other person sour.

Recognizing the Right Time

Just as people give clues when their receptivity is low, they give clues when their receptivity is high or when your timing is correct—the right time. When the other person begins to express approval for some part of what you have said, it is an indication that the time is right to express your point of view.

Another way that people reflect their interest and indicate that it's the right time, is by asking questions. Examples of questions that indicate interest or a high level of receptivity are, "Where can I find this?" "What is your opinion on this?", "How do you feel about the change?", "Is there anything else I have to do?", "What else are you going to do?" Those are only a few samples of the many possible questions that might be asked, which indicate a high level of receptivity and the "Right Time."

Tips on Keeping the "Right Time"

The way to keep the "Right Time" is to be considerate of the other person and show that you are really interested in his opinions and comments. One way to do this is to do it non-verbally. When conversing, especially when the other person is talking, lean forward toward the person who is speaking. Nod your head to show that you are listening, look into the speaker's eyes, and smile occasionally. These positive reinforcements will keep the other person's receptivity high and your timing right.

The primary method for keeping the "Right Time," is to use question sets that keep the other person talking, but guide his remarks to the area you want to discuss. A question set is a set of questions all of which are related to a specific topic. One topic might be a location, another work, the economy, social issues, philosophy, etc. These questions can also be used just to keep a conversation going.

The following standard questions may be adapted to any topic of importance.

"How do you feel about . . .?"
"What type is it . . .?"
"What do you think of the . . . (economy)?"
"How did you react to . . .?"
"When will these conditions improve?"
"Why do you think this occurred?"
"Who do you think is most influential in . . .?"
"Where is the best place to get . . .?"
"What do you think caused this?"
"What is the most important aspect of this?"

How to Say It Right When the Time Is Right

One of the greatest salesmen I have ever met seemed to be able to say the right thing in the right way at any time under any circumstances. Once he was trying to sell a load of frozen turkeys to a chain store buyer. A new method had been developed in which the wing tips and necks were removed from the turkey before freezing. In his presentation, he pointed out the savings to the consumer who no longer had to pay for the neck and wing tips.

Unknown to the salesman the system had been changed. The wing tips were removed but the neck was put back inside the package. When a sample was opened for the customer, there for all to see was a neck. "Look," said the customer, "The consumer is going to have to pay for a neck that she can't use." "Oh! No," replied the salesman, "she can use the neck to make gravy."

For those who are not as adept at using humor, a more cautious approach is necessary. The following rules will help you say it right when the time is right.

1. State your point as an opinion not an irrefutable fact.
2. Be flexible enough to change a minor point to protect your major view.
3. Pause so that your ideas may be absorbed and commented upon.
4. Ask questions to ensure understanding
5. Summarize your main points.

By following those five rules, you will find that people will more often agree with you than usual. By stating your point as an opinion, you are less likely to irritate people who hold minor differences of opinion. If they are not irritated, they are more likely to alter their view and accept your position.

By being flexible yourself, you encourage the other person to also be flexible. By pausing, you permit the other person time to absorb and respond, which aids understanding. By asking questions, you determine whether your ideas are really accepted or not. By summarizing your main point, you remind the other person that all the evidence you presented was meant to support those particular points.

How Wendy Scanlon Used *"Conversational Timing"* to Win a Popularity Contest

Wendy Scanlon was running for homecoming queen and wanted to win. Wendy developed her own brand of "Conversational Timing" to win this popularity contest. She made speeches, visited sororities, and talked to everyone who would listen. Wendy won the contest and when asked how she did it, itemized the following conversational techniques.

1. Carefully listen to people's opinions.
2. Ask questions that encourage others to speak.
3. Summarize serious ideas and opinions.
4. Offer opinions rather than irrefutable facts.
5. Discuss new topics that interest the other person.
6. Maintain humor.
7. Be tolerant and accept criticism cheerfully.
8. Be prepared with three or four topics to discuss.
9. Show friendliness with idle chit-chat.
10. Never argue with anyone.

9

Conversational Short-Cuts to Popularity

Over a long period of time, popularity is dependent upon personality traits that are pleasing to other people. In the short run, however, you can quickly establish popularity using a few conversational short-cuts. These short-cuts will help make an initial favorable impression. After the initial impression, your basic personality traits will carry you.

In this chapter, you'll learn the secrets of winning friends, entertaining others, holding people's interest, approaching people at parties, and introducing interesting topics of conversation at work. You can use these secret techniques as short-cuts in building your popularity. As you use them, they will begin to feel natural to you, and you will use them without thought. Eventually your personality will show improvement, and you will win long term popularity.

HOW TO USE CONVERSATIONAL SHORT-CUTS TO GET PEOPLE TO LIKE YOU

The secret of gaining popularity is in relating to the interests of the people you talk to. Although people like many things and these vary with each person, everyone has a number of basic areas of interest that are similar. You can relate to and ask questions about these basic interests in your short-cut approach to gaining popularity.

The Conversation Tree

One short-cut method of gaining popularity is to use the conversational tree. The tree is simply a memory device that you tie to the person you are talking to, to help you remember to relate to the areas of interest of the person you are talking to. You picture the person as a tree. His legs and feet become the roots of the tree, his body the trunk, his arms the branches and his head the top of the tree.

Once you set the picture up in your mind, you can easily relate basic areas of interest to the person you're talking to and by just glaring at different sections of his or her body, you'll be reminded to talk or ask questions about that area of interest. First, it seems logical to think of the roots of the tree (legs of the man) as the roots of the man. The man's legs or feet will be reminders to ask or talk about his origin. You may ask where he was born, lived, moved from or to, grew up, etc. This could cover a person's early childhood. You could also ask about his line of descent, where his parents come from, their culture and heritage, etc.

Next, the trunk of the tree (the body of the man) should remind you of the major development of the man. His growth, the schools he attended, his accomplishments in preparing for life. The major skills he has acquired and how he has used them. These are things that form the foundation for life and include hobbies and recreation as well as home and friends. This area alone could keep you talking for hours.

Finally, there is the top of the tree (the head of man). This is the knowledge area. The area of philosophy, beliefs, convictions and the goals the individual strives for. This is the area of politics, religion, economics, law, the area of moral and ethical consideration. If there is a pet grievance against society or the world, it is just cause for conversation.

You can keep the conversation going by using the conversational tree to renew topics of interest. To really become popular, however, you must listen carefully to what the other

person says. You must listen and try to understand. For it is not through talking that you gain popularity but rather through listening and understanding.

The Secret of Winning New Friends

The short-cut secret of winning new friends is to always find something good to say. You can talk about the weather, the scenery or work, but whatever you talk about be positive. If you don't feel good, don't take it out on the other person. No one wants to hear people complain, so don't. If you always find something good to say, it will improve your own outlook also. You won't slip into a rut and see the worst in every situation. In fact, in time you'll actually see some good in worst situations.

Also, find something good to say about the person you're talking to. If you look closely, this will be easy. An article of clothing, a new hair style or any change in dress or manner of dress. People change because they think it makes them look better. If they do look better, tell them so.

Characteristics of a Good Friend

A good friend helps a friend. He builds up rather than belittles. He encourages, helps and persuades you to be better and do better in life. A friend knows that what you send out to others always comes back to you. There is a story about a small boy who became so angry with his mother that he ran out of the house yelling "I hate you, I hate you." It happened that conditions were just right for an echo and the boy heard coming back to him "I hate you, I hate you."

He ran into the house and told his mother, "There's a bad little boy out there yelling that he hates me." The mother told her son to go back and try yelling, "I love you, I love you" and see what happened. In a few moments the boy had yelled, heard his answer and was back in the house, all smiles.

Zig Zigler, a famous speaker, tells the impact a few good words had on him as a young salesman. Mr. Zigler did not believe in himself; he did not think he could sell. Eventually, his boss told him that he had watched him for two and a half years and knew that Zig had the makings of a great salesman. He pointed out all the attributes that would make him great and ended by saying, "You can be great, if you believe in yourself and go to work." Zig got the message, went to work, and became first a great salesman and later a great speaker. He attributes his success to those early words of encouragement. What greater friend could you ever have than one who encourages you to grow and succeed as a person.

How John Kingsley Gained Popularity in Seven Days

John Kingsley was a transfer student to a new school. He had no friends and had to begin a difficult study schedule in seven days. John decided to use the time to build his popularity and win friends. John worked out a seven-day plan and began working to build his popularity.

The first day, John engaged in casual conversation. He learned the background and goals of his fellow students. He made acquaintances, but he let them do most of the talking while he listened.

The second day, he tried to show himself as an average guy. He was careful not to seem arrogant or self-righteous. He avoided pompous or stuffy language and tried to speak in a quiet, friendly way.

On the third day, John expressed his opinions but was careful not to come on too strong. He expressed them as opinions, not as irrefutable facts. He was careful to listen to other points of view and avoided argument.

The fourth day was spent in selecting specific friends, people he found who had similar likes with those of his own. He made an effort to spend additional time with them and asked questions to learn more about their interests.

On the fifth day, John spent his time saying good things. All day, he made an effort to concentrate on the positive. He made cheerful comments and paid compliments. If he couldn't find something to compliment, he said something cheerful about the weather or the scenery.

John spent the sixth day quietly listening to others. He listened to what they said and watched how they acted toward him. He watched their facial expressions and listened to their voices to see if they were or were not friendly. He found them to be friendly.

On the seventh day John acted natural. He was friendly and found that he could naturally follow the steps he had developed to win popularity. John was satisfied that his plan had worked and knew that he had gained the popularity and friendship he desired.

THREE WAYS TO BE POPULAR AT PARTIES

Parties are meant to be fun. People can join in friendly conversation, have a good time and not generally be concerned about making a formal impression. For those who feel ill at ease or can't think of anything to say, however, a party can be a devastating experience. The three ways to be popular covered in this section will help overcome those problems.

Five Conversational Techniques That Hold Interest at Parties

There are certain people who always seem to hold everyone's interest at parties. They are popular and are sought out more often than the average person. A recent study revealed five basic techniques that are repeatedly used by the most interesting people at parties. The techniques are not all used by any particular person, rather they are the different techniques used by a number of different people.

The five techniques are: (1) Tune in to the other person's area of expertise. (2) Become an expert in some topic of interest. (3) Keep abreast of current research findings. (4) Memorize historical events. (5) Check the newspaper each day for current events.

Tune in to the other person's area of expertise. Nearly everyone has some area of expertise. One person may be an expert in sports, another in music, another in electronics, and another in books or movies. The most popular people at parties are the ones who discover others' areas of expertise and encourage them to talk. They question the people they talk to and listen carefully to the answer.

When the other person's answer reflects excitement, or a change in voice tone or rate of speech, we may assume that an area of interest has been discovered. At this point more questions of the "how," "why," and "tell me more" variety are used. These questions show interest and respect for the expertise of the other person. He appreciates the interest, attention, and respect, and the person who did the questioning and listening gains respect and increased popularity.

Become an expert in some topic of interest. One way to continue to be interesting to others is to become an expert in some area that is either unusual or is generally interesting to a large number of people. For example, a sport such as baseball or football is interesting to a large number of people. A few hours a week with books from the library complimented with the daily news and you're on your way to becoming an expert in sports.

To find a unique area to become an expert in, you might spend a few hours searching through the library to find an unusual yet interesting topic. As you look, ask yourself, "Will this be interesting to other people?" Once you find a topic that fits all your requirements, begin your program of learning. Remember your objective is to become an expert, not just to acquaint yourself with the topic.

You must learn the details of the topic that are not generally known to laymen. For example, suppose you decide to become an expert wine taster. You must learn the language and details of wine tasting. You need to learn the definition and taste of the words, *complete, round* and *body.* You must learn to evaluate the appearance, the smell, and the taste of wine in order to become an expert. A library, some practice, and perhaps a wine tasting course and you're on your way to becoming an expert.

Keep abreast of current research findings. Newspaper and magazine articles frequently report research findings because anything new is news. These new findings are interesting and are always welcome topics of conversation. By spending a few minutes each day looking through newspapers and magazines, you'll find all the new research findings you need. You'll be surprised how much there is when you look for it.

For example recent research findings indicate that college students rank *family, friendship, purpose in life* and *being successful* higher than did non-college students of the same age.

The non-college students ranked *steady work, chances for advancement, chances to make lots of money* and *having lots of money* higher than did college students of the same age. Isn't it ironic that those less likely to earn lots of money, value it more highly.

Memorize historical events. You may not be aware of the widespread use of historical events in everyday conversation. People consistently use historical information to support an idea or draw a parallel to a current event. You can make your own list of historical events and use the picture association system to memorize them. For a starter, you might wish to memorize the following list.

1492	Columbus discovered America
1564	Shakespeare was born
1607	First English settlement in America—Jamestown
1776	Declaration of Independence
1789	Destruction of the Bastille
1807	Robert E. Lee was born
1819	Queen Victoria was born
1830	Revolution in France
1914	First World War
1941	Second World War
1950	Korean War
1964	Vietnam War

Check the newspaper each day for current events. A large portion of the conversation that takes place each day is related to current events. Check the paper each day for topics of interest so that you can respond to the comments that are made throughout the day to current events. You might want to remember an item from each category in the paper. You could, for example, memorize one national, one state, and one local event each day. That way you will be prepared to at least comment on any of the three that comes up.

How to Retain Your Poise at Parties

We often find ourselves facing hostile or unexpected embarassing situations at parties. Some people seem to handle unexpected situations with grace and charm and never seem to lose their poise. Nothing seems to bother them. They retain their balance and keep control of the situation, they do not become emotionally involved, and they almost always react in an impersonal, rational way.

Retaining your poise at parties simply means keeping your cool. Be prepared to face an impolite remark from some unexpected source. Ignore the remark if you can; if not, simply comment that you can see the person who spoke is having a lot of fun.

The key to retaining your poise is to show that you are an understanding person and realize that people are just having fun. If you indicate that you think everything is said in jest or is said innocently, then there is no reason to become emotional. You don't have to defend yourself or criticize the other person. You can keep your cool and retain your poise.

How to Overcome Shyness at Parties

If you are a shy person, it is probably related to how you feel about yourself. Recent studies have shown that people are reluctant to speak out or make contact with other people because they fear they will seem silly or say something that seems to show ignorance or a lack of knowledge. Even well-educated people are afraid to speak because of a fear of not expressing themselves well or a fear that their opinions will not be popular.

The shy person can learn to overcome shyness, become less passive and more popular at parties by developing a positive feeling about himself. To develop a positive feeling you must improve your self-esteem. People with low self-esteem usually have compared themselves with unrealistic models. Those with high self-esteem, on the other hand, take a more realistic view of themselves. They compare themselves with people at their own level, not with people who are in superior or more advanced positions.

Ten Steps Toward Overcoming Shyness

The following ten steps were developed to guide shy people very slowly through a process of identifying, isolating, and overcoming those situations that cause shyness. This system may be helpful for people who are not shy in overcoming other problems.

1. Make a list of situations that cause you to feel shy. You may need to work on this list for a week or more to make sure you get every situation listed that causes you to feel uncertain or shy. Think of past events and list them as well as the ones you encounter during the week. Write down all you can think of, the major and the smallest minor situations. Add any circumstance that has caused or any one that you think would cause you to feel shy. It is important to find all the minor situations as well as the major ones, as they will be used in later steps to overcome your shyness.

2. *Make a list of people who cause you to feel shy.* Though you may not have thought about it, very often it's the people who cause you to feel shy rather than the situation. It may be that there is one particular person who crowds you in some way and makes you feel shy. One person may be overly critical, another may be pushy, or another may be trying to manipulate you. Any of these or other impolite behaviors may be responsible for shyness. Again, list the people who only have a minor effect on your shyness as well as the ones who have a major effect.

3. *Rank the situations and the people in terms of the impact they have on your shyness.* The ranking should include both the situations and the people combined on the same list. The idea here is to get the most difficult or the major cause of shyness, whether that be a situation or a person at the top of #1 spot on the list. Then the next most difficult would be listed as #2, then #3, etc. The last person or situation on the list would be one that would cause very little difficulty or shyness.

4. *Prepare a list of small steps to overcome your shyness.* The secret to overcoming shyness (and the reason for ranking in step (3) is to take very small steps toward openness and away from shyness. Select the largest number on your list (the least difficult person or situation) as a goal for the first small step. This step should be one that you feel generally comfortable with, but one that occasionally causes you to feel shy.

The next step would be very slightly more difficult. You should practice each step until you feel comfortable before going on to the next one. Continue your list with each level being a little more difficult then the preceding one until you have listed all the difficult situations and people that cause you to become shy.

5. *Work toward more and more difficult goals.* What you are trying to do is to desensitize yourself to the difficult situa-

tions that cause you to feel and act shy. If you tried to overcome the most difficult situation first, you would most likely fail.

Caution: You may encounter some failure during the first few steps. This simply indicates you are going too fast. Back up and repeat the previous step, and then practice the next step alone before trying it at a party.

As you move through each step, you will feel better and better about yourself and your ability to talk and mingle at parties without shyness. Eventually you will lose all your shyness, will feel comfortable in all situations, and will automatically be more popular and have more fun at parties.

6. Accept negative criticism without resentment. Never resent constructive criticism. Remember that we all make mistakes and that we can learn from those mistakes. There's nothing wrong in making mistakes as long as we learn from them. So be gracious when you are criticized. This doesn't mean that you have to accept insults. Don't let people belittle you by calling you names. There's nothing to be learned from insults. Legitimate criticism is leveled at statements or actions, not at people.

7. Practice to correct errors. Have you ever left a party and thought of a number of things that you could have said? Did people say things that you should have had an answer for but didn't, then you thought of all the answers later? The way to handle these situations is to prepare for them by practicing in advance.

Write things down that are said that you wish to respond to. Then set up two chairs and role-play the situation. Sit in one chair and pretend you are the other person. Make a comment that he would be most likely to say. Then move to the other chair and think to yourself, "What would I say if I were not shy?" Take all the time you need to think up an answer. Once you think it, say it out loud. Move back and forth between the two chairs and practice until you feel comfortable in any situation. As you practice, you will begin to think of answers faster and will eventually think of answers fast enough for any conversation.

8. Compliment yourself for success. Remember that the reason most people are shy is that they don't have confidence in themselves. Therefore, it is important to build a series of small successes to prove to yourself that you are overcoming your shyness. One way to convince yourself is to compliment yourself out loud. Say, "I said the right thing," or, "I was not shy, I was popular at the party." These compliments will help you begin to feel good about yourself; you will become more and more open and less and less shy.

9. Pick realistic models to emulate. Most people pick a model at some time in their life and then they try to emulate that person. You may pick a model to emulate that you are unable to copy. The individual may be too far advanced. No matter how hard you try you will not be able to accomplish the same things your model does.

If you realize that your model is too far advanced for you to emulate, select a new less advanced model to avoid a serious problem. Many times a person doesn't realize that his model is an unrealistic one, and he keeps trying to emulate the model. He fails, of course, and forms a low opinion of himself. This low opinion results in shyness.

You can avoid or overcome this problem by making sure that anyone you try to emulate is not too far advanced for you to copy. If your goals are realistic, you will be able to obtain them with reasonable effort. If they are not realistic, you will only become depressed or lose confidence in yourself.

10. Go to a party. Now that you have developed a plan to overcome your shyness and have practiced the first few steps, go to a party. I don't mean to go to a party with the intention of not being shy, I mean go to a party to learn how other people act at parties. Once you get there, listen and make a mental note of the kinds of things they talk about.

This experience will help you overcome your shyness. Once you see how ordinary most conversation is, you will feel much more qualified to speak up yourself. After the party, continue your step-by-step improvement plan until you can go to another party without any shyness at all.

Connie Blaine's Short-Cut Rise to Popularity

Connie Blaine was married to an outgoing, well-educated engineer. Her husband had achieved a number of successes at work, and although Connie was proud of her husband, she began to feel more and more unsure of herself. She had always been a little shy and became even more so when her husband joined people in conversations about philosophy or engineering, subjects which she knew nothing about.

Finally Connie talked to a counselor about her problem. The counselor advised her to stop comparing herself to her husband. Connie had selected her husband as a model to emulate, and he was an unrealistic model. She could not expect to talk about technical or advanced subjects that she had not been educated for. She should concentrate, she was told, on current events or community items that held special interest for her.

Connie slowly changed. She stopped trying to talk about subjects she did not understand and began to study local and national news events. She very rapidly gained a great deal of information on local politics, national events, and sports.

Connie started with one small step. She began to talk local politics with one of her close friends. She was very careful not to get into a conversation with her husband about local politics because he was one of the people who created the difficult situations for her.

She expanded the number of people she talked local politics to, until she began to feel very comfortable talking about politics with anyone. Finally she began to talk politics with her husband. He was surprised that she knew more about local politics than he did and gave her the encouragement and self-confidence to discuss other topics. Soon she was one of the best informed and one of the most popular women in the neighborhood. Connie (not her real name) is now councilwoman in a small western city.

10

Conversational Magic
That Wins New Friends

Many people form few friendships because they are hesitant to talk to new people. Other people fail to form friendships, in spite of their attempts at conversation, because their speaking habits do not inspire trust. Both these common problems are shared by millions of people. These problems can be overcome by using the concepts shared in this chapter. By practicing the concepts each day, you will soon feel comfortable speaking with new people and will be using Conversational Magic to win new friends.

HOW CONVERSATIONAL MAGIC
WINS PEOPLE'S TRUST

Recent research studies have shown that trustworthiness (the ability and willingness to keep confidence) along with loyalty and warmth are the most important qualities of friendship. The same study found that betrayal of a confidence was most often the cause of ending a friendship. Other elements that people in the study identified as important friendship factors are supportiveness, a willingness to share personal time, a sense of humor, willingness to talk frankly, and a social conscience.

Five Conversational Techniques
That Build Trust

The following five techniques have been found to be effective in winning trust and respect from people in all situations. By using these methods you can develop new friends, and by remaining loyal, you can retain those friends for as long as you wish.

1. Be open and free in expressing your feelings. In one study over 80% of the men and women respondents identified open, free intimate talk as an element of friendship. You need not share your innermost secrets, but a willingness to express your honest feelings about the topics you discuss is important in winning friends.

2. Don't be aggressive. If you are too forward or aggressive in your early contact with people, you will scare them away. Most people rebel against aggressiveness. They want their own space and want time to understand you and see how you react to the different aspects of their personality. They want to determine if the two of you have anything in common.

3. Don't be an all-subject expert. Many people are irritated and turned off by people who know everything about everything. So, don't present your opinions and ideas as irrefutable fact. Point out that you are expressing your own point of view and would be interested in hearing the other person's opinion on the same topic. This builds respect because it shows that you are interested in and respect the other person's opinion.

4. Develop good listening habits. Friends listen to each other. There's not much value in a friendship when only one person listens. To develop meaningful friendships, show your willingness to listen to the person you wish to become your friend. It's not enough *just to listen.* You must listen carefully and empathetically to show the other person that you are listening. Make comments and ask questions related to the topic the other person is talking about. You have to be listening to ask a question or make a comment related to the topic of discussion.

5. Express warmth and trust with your voice. Researchers have found that people who speak in a quiet, relaxed way are perceived by their listeners as having warmth, empathy, and sincerity. You can develop this speech style by practicing. Speak into a tape recorder and purposely speak slower and slower each time. Alter the tone of your voice until it is in a middle range, not too rough, not too high pitched. Don't overdo this so that your voice is strained. Always strive for a relaxed feeling when you speak.

A quiet, relaxed voice can demonstrate trust even in critical situations. A mother recently told how she always used a quiet, relaxed, trusting tone in her voice. She said, for example, that once when she heard a lot of noise downstairs where her daughter was entertaining her boyfriend, the mother called down, "What are you doing daughter?" The daughter, with a slip of the tongue, called back, "We're here in the loving room, mother." The mother attempted to trustfully correct the daughter with, "That's *living* daughter." The daughter replied, "It sure is, mother." That's trust!

How a Lonely Girl Used Conversational Magic to Win New Friends

Linda Jacobs said she had been lonely for as long as she could remember. She was lonely in grade school, high school and college. Now she was working and was still lonely. Linda decided to do something about her loneliness and after consultation began a program designed to make friends. Linda began talking to anyone and everyone who would listen. She soon discovered the people who were giving and attending parties and spent as much time as possible talking to them.

When a secret or confidence was revealed, Linda was quick to say that she could be trusted. She pointed out that she could keep a confidence and would never reveal a secret entrusted to her. Soon Linda was being invited to parties and she began to make friends.

Linda listened carefully to those with whom she was trying to develop friendships. She was patient, empathetic, and friendly. She asked for other's opinions and really listened to their answers. She found that she could make friends easily and she continued to do so. Soon Linda had many friends, was always busy, and forgot that she had ever been lonely. Today Linda is one of the most popular girls in her office.

CONVERSATIONAL TECHNIQUES THAT BUILD RESPECT

There are many ways to build respect. People will respect skill, knowledge, money, honesty, courtesy, integrity, etc. Those traits are not easy to display, however. They reveal themselves only over a period of time. In the long run, you will gain respect from these traits, but in the short run you may apply more easily demonstrated traits. Laughter and the use of quotations are two techniques that can be used to build respect very quickly.

How Laughter Affects Personal Respect

Have you ever thought that the things you laugh at reflect an aspect of your personality. Recent research has shown that what you laugh at is a reflection of how you feel at the time (whether you are happy or depressed) and that the category of jokes you find most funny reflects an inner conflict or deep concern about the content or theme of the joke. If you analyze your favorite joke, you will probably realize that you have some concern about the theme or the punch line of the joke.

If you want to win respect with laughter, learn to laugh at yourself. See the irony in the frustrations you encounter; recognize these frustrations as trivial irritations that are part of life. Laugh at your tendency to get mad—laugh at yourself and you will win respect.

Laughter is like poise, it is valuable in times of stress. When you feel irritated or upset, just remember to laugh. In addition to being ready to laugh at yourself, you can also develop respect by developing humorous puns. Research studies have shown that a person who develops humorous puns is more likely to be a happy, well-adjusted person.

Since people are different in their hang-ups and their areas of concern, they will laugh at different jokes. See *Psychology Today's* "Different Jokes for Different Folks," by Hassett and Houlihan, in the January 1979 issue.

The secret, then, of developing funny puns, is to remember a few one liners and change them to fit the subject. The topic of conversation will most often relate to an area of interest of the people you are talking to. It is best to wait until the conversation is light in nature before trying a pun. If you have not used puns in the past, try them first with your family and friends. Only when you have practiced enough to feel comfortable using them, should you try puns with groups of people. For examples of puns related to various subjects, see *Braude's Treasury of Wit and Humor,* Prentice-Hall, 1978.

How Quotations Build Respect

Quotations can be memorized and used to build respect, provided they are in good taste and are used to support a point or illustrate an idea or opinion. Memorize a number of quotations and use them as appropriate.

One way to prepare to use quotations is to list the major issues of the day, then look through a book of quotations and find one that expresses your point of view on each issue. As with humorous puns, you should only use quotations in public after you have first practiced them with friends and feel comfortable with them.

Joan Watney's Rise to Popularity with New Friends

Joan Watney started building her popularity by building respect with quotations. Joan believed that women would have to work harder than men to get promoted. She often expressed her views to women and men and decided to gather quotations to support her views.

She quoted Hamilton: "All the genius I have is merely the fruit of labor." Then, Carlyle: "Genius is the capacity for taking infinite pains." And, Michelangelo: "If people knew how hard I work to get my mastery, it wouldn't seem so wonderful after all." Finally, Edison: "Genius is one per cent inspiration and ninety-nine per cent perspiration."

By using quotations that were appropriate to her point of view, Joan very quickly gained the respect of her friends and acquaintances. Her popularity led to new acquiantances, a rise in popularity, and many new friends.

HOW TO USE CONVERSATIONAL MAGIC
TO TURN ACQUAINTANCES INTO FRIENDS

From your acquaintances, you may select those whom you would like as friends. The selection process is mutual, however, and you must be selected just as you select. In order to form a favorable impression, speak in non-critical terms, avoid argument, and improve your own disposition.

Speak in Non-Critical Terms

We generally are not aware of the impact our words have on other people. When we tell others "you're wrong," "you shouldn't" "you should," or similar messages tied to the word *you,* we appear to be criticizing the other person.

Messages that start with the word "you" or contain it and give a negative connotation will be ineffective. These "you-oriented" critical messages are ineffective because they make people feel guilty, stupid, rejected, unloved, angry.

Obviously if a person has these guilty or "put down" feelings, he will not be listening to or trying to understand you. If you want to make friends and still get your message across, you must avoid combining your message with criticism.

To get your message across, without creating the obstacles that result from guilt, anger, or feelings of being put down, structure your messages in such a way that you avoid the "you-orientation." *The way to avoid speaking in a critical way to the other person, is to tell the other your feelings about what has occurred.*

Rather than telling your brother, sister, or child: "You're making too much noise," say: "I feel upset with all the noise." None of us, normally, wish to do things that upset, irritate or anger other people. By simply stating our feelings, without criticism, we give the other person the opportunity to correct his behavior without losing his pride. He is not being forced to stop, he is stopping because he has concern for the feelings of others.

To Develop Friendship, Avoid Argument

It is important to understand the impact our verbal behavior (our words) have on others. We can intensify the frustration the other person feels by arguing or being critical of him. We may actually be responsible for the hostile behavior a teenager or small child exhibits.

Suppose a child is trying to repair his bike. He has made two or three false starts and is frustrated because he has not finished. The parent yells out to the child: "How long are you going to be 'goofing around' with the bike?" This criticism may have a very strong effect on the child. Not only is he frustrated for the lack of progress in repairing the bike, but now he is being accused of "goofing off." This criticism may be the "last straw" that will cause the child to blow his stack. A "non-critical" or an "I message" would have been more appropriate.

When you take exception with what someone—a father, mother, child, brother, sister, friend—says, be aware of the impact of your words. If you argue or indicate the other person is wrong, you force him to take a protective stand. In his effort to protect himself, he will search his mind for statements to defend his position. These statements will probably be biased and reflect the prejudices upon which the original statement was based.

During this protective process, his mind will be closed. All his thoughts will be directed towards proving himself right, which incidentally, also means proving you wrong. You are now the enemy. There may be much more latitude taken in proving you wrong. Since you attacked his credibility, he may now attack yours.

No matter how long the argument goes on, you will not be able to get him to open his mind. As a matter of fact, the longer you argue the less chance you will have of getting him to listen. Why? Because you are asking him to contradict his original statement.

The other person's self-esteem need not be threatened when you disagree with him. Just as he stated his position, you may state yours. To avoid threatening or criticizing, however, state your arguments in terms of how you think and feel. *You should state your beliefs in terms of being your ideas and opinions, not as being unchallengeable laws.*

By avoiding the pitfall of argument, you retain his friendship. There can be no argument over your right to think, feel, or believe as you choose. There also is no challenge to the other person's rights. He may believe as he chooses. If both people abide by these principles, friendship will naturally follow from the relationship.

Improve Your Own Disposition

Obviously, the more pleasing personality or better disposition you have, the more friends you will have. The four following guidelines will help you improve your own disposition and win more friends.

1. Don't give advice. The only time you are safe in giving advice is when someone specifically requests it. Generally people see advice as criticism. Since advice by its nature is intended to be a better way of doing things, people often feel that you are criticizing the way they are currently doing things.

If you persist in giving advice, you not only will find it difficult to make new friends, you will rapidly lose your old ones. You can determine this for yourself by simply asking people before you offer advice. If you ask, "Would you like some advice?" you'll be surprised at the number of people who answer "No!" In a survey I conducted, more than eight out of ten people replied "No."

2. Be courteous. Friendship is based on trust, respect, and a willingness to share time. Part of sharing time is being courteous. A willingness to listen, to try to understand and sympathize, is part of courtesy. Don't be rude or put down your friend. Friends want you to be candid but in a polite way, so say what you have to say but do it without criticism. Speak of the situation, not the person. Don't say, "You did a dumb thing." Say, "That didn't turn out too well."

3. Let people feel important. Friends need support, and the way to support them is to let them feel important. To do this ask them questions; ask for their opinions; ask for their suggestions. Once you ask, listen carefully. Let them explain in full detail. The more they talk, the more important they feel.

Especially ask about topics that your friend has expertise in. Everyone likes to talk about his own area of expertise. It gives him an opportunity to show how much he really knows and helps him feel important. If you learn to make other people feel important, you'll soon have more friends than you have time to listen to.

4. *Show your appreciation for favors.* Many people go through life accepting favors but never showing appreciation for them. This is often true of children who were constantly given things by their parents. After a number of years of having their parents take care of everything for them, they begin to expect it. When they are adults and someone does them a favor, they feel they deserve it. They begin to expect favors from others just as they did from their parents.

Although I believe each person must learn to do for himself and stand on his own feet, everyone needs help or a favor occasionally. When you do receive a favor, remember it and show your appreciation. Thank the person who helped you and as the years go by let the people who helped you know that you remember and still appreciate their help. This will assure you of lifelong friendship.

How a Quiet Employee Won Respect and Friendship on a New Job

Gary was a quiet employee who did his job well but had no friends. On one particularly slow day, Gary became caught up with all his work and wanted someone to talk to. As Gary looked around the office, he realized for the first time that he had no friends. He wanted friends and began to wonder why he had none.

Gary asked himself these questions:

"Why do I not have friends?"
"What have I done wrong?"
"What can I do to make friends?"

As Gary pondered these questions, he realized that he had to listen to others to find out what they needed, what it took to be a friend. Larry sensed that friends fill each others' needs for trust, confidentiality, and support. He became a good listener and avoided criticism. He commented on the events and the situations surrounding the events but did not criticize the person involved.

Gary learned to be supportive and let the other person feel important. Gary paid sincere compliments where they were deserved. He became more observant of how his new-found friends dressed and complimented them when they deserved it.

Flattery was avoided by Gary. He knew that sincerity is more than just signing your letters "sincerely yours." Gary complimented people only when they deserved it for their ideas, opinions, or actions.

Gary thought well and expected the best of people. He was tolerant and patient. He didn't expect everyone to jump at becoming his friend immediately; he knew that building friendships takes time. Gary realized that friendship is a commitment to loyalty in thought and action. He was willing to share his time with others to build that friendship.

Gary's efforts paid off. In three months he had more friends than anyone in the office. No one remembers the old quiet Gary. Everyone remembers and appreciates the new Gary—their friend.

11

How to Use
Conversational Magic
to Win Support

Everyone needs the support of other people. Whether on-the-job, at home, or in a social group, no one can stand alone in all things. Certain projects, by their very nature, require co-operation, and to get cooperation, to get people to support you, you need to use the techniques of persuasion.

In this chapter you'll learn the conversational techniques that get people to listen to and support your ideas. You'll see how to deal with people who ordinarily won't listen, and you'll learn, by example, how to win support for your ideas and plans.

THE CONVERSATIONAL KEYS THAT
GET PEOPLE TO LISTEN TO YOUR IDEAS

The keys to getting people to listen to your ideas are:

1. Show how your idea will benefit your listener.
2. Show how your idea fits your listener's previously held convictions.
3. Avoid emotion-laden issues.
4. Deal with issues, not personalities.
5. Listen carefully and don't counterargue.

Show How Your Idea
Will Benefit Your Listener

People are always interested in ideas from which they can benefit. Whether the benefit is financial, fun, or health, when you mention one of these benefits, you catch your listener's attention. A lead-in such as, "This will help you improve . . ." or, "you can increase . . ." or, "you will gain . . ." will catch the attention and interest of your listener.

For example, if you're trying to convince a friend to go swimming with you, you may either talk about the fun of swimming or the health aspects of swimming. If you want your listener to make a contribution to a charity that you favor, point out how the work the charity does will benefit your listener. This might be the development of a better community, less crime, fewer people depending upon public support, etc.

If your listener does not find the benefit you mention appealing, he will tell you so. When this happens, simply pick another benefit. Everyone is interested in something, and with a few trials you'll be able to find your listener's area of interest. Once you know his area of interest, you can relate the benefits of your idea to that interest.

Show How Your Idea Fits Your Listener's
Previously Held Convictions

If people are aware that the idea you express is consistent with other ideas they hold or with convictions they have previously developed, they will accept your idea. Often people don't see this connection, however, and you must point it out. People generally hold a number of similar ideas or a "set" of beliefs and convictions. They form new convictions by generalizing from the "set." If you can logically show that your idea fits the "set" of convictions of your listener, he will accept your idea because he feels comfortable with ideas similar to his own.

A local college girl who wanted to get a job in a restaurant after class, confronted her father who did not want her to work. The girl knew that her father believed that young people should take part in family social activities as a means of developing poise and social skills. The girl pointed out to her father that working as a waitress would help her develop social skills and poise. The father, seeing the logic of an idea that fit his own beliefs, permitted her to take the job.

Avoid Emotion-Laden Issues

A sure way to turn your listener off, block understanding, and cut off listening is to try to convince someone to change his view about a long-standing emotional issue. Although people hold many issues so dear that they become emotional over them, two are universally prone to emotionalism. These two are religion and politics. The only way to avoid argument about religion and politics is to remain completely neutral. Never argue about either. You can listen to another's comments; you don't have to agree but don't argue.

Deal with Issues Not Personalities

In winning support for your plans and ideas, stick to the issues. Often you will encounter opposition based on personal preferences and desires. People may introduce extraneous issues, prejudiced remarks, and opinionated bias. The natural human instinct is to attack the personality involved. This form of conversation, although ego-satisfying, actually works against your objective.

Your objective is to win support for your ideas or the issues you favor. If you stick to the issues and keep providing evidence to support those issues, your evidence will make a positive impression on your listener. Your opponents, who depend upon personality-based arguments, will leave a negative impression. Eventually your point of view will prevail, and you will be remembered as a calm, rational, ethical person.

Listen Carefully and Don't Counterargue

One of the most valuable techniques in getting support for your point of view is to thoroughly understand opposing viewpoints. To do this, you must listen carefully and never counterargue. Most people, however, when they hear an opposing view, argue rather than try to understand. If you think about this procedure, you will realize that to overcome opposing ideas, you must thoroughly understand them. Remember to avoid argument and ask questions in order to gain the understanding that permits you to develop evidence to overcome the opposing view.

How Harry Blems, a Salesman, Got a New Owner to Listen to His Sales Presentation

Harry Blems had called on a very "hardheaded" prospect for nearly twenty years but was never able to get an order. Finally the man passed away. Harry heard about his demise, and that the man's wife was taking over the business. Harry also heard that after thirty years of living with her "hard headed" husband, the wife had become very defensive and she too was difficult to sell. Harry called on the widow and went through his entire presentation. Harry specified all the benefits of his products, showed that his products fit the image of the store, and asked the widow for an order. She hesitated a minute, then said, "I don't see any of your products here in the store. Didn't my husband buy your products?" Harry smilingly responded, "As you probably know, your late husband was a little hard headed!" He got the order.

HOW TO DEAL WITH PEOPLE WHO DON'T LISTEN TO YOU

People don't listen because they are preoccupied with other thoughts. Those thoughts are related to some topic of interest, and you must find something more interesting or give your listener some reason to listen to you. The following approach will help you establish a listening climate.

How to Establish a Favorable Listening Climate

When we start to talk to someone, our first few words establish the climate. In effect the unsaid part of the message comes across loud and clear. It says: "This is how we're going to deal with each other." Or it says: "This is how I'm going to deal with you."

Let's suppose, for example, that a teen-ager wants to use the family car one night a week. He is going to bring the subject up at the dinner table. What he says and how he says it, perhaps the very first sentence, will set the climate for the discussions. A demand or a sarcastic remark will establish a climate for a fight. Here's an example of this type, where our teen-ager, let's call him Bill, approaches his father.

"Dad, I want the car on Friday nights. I have a date every Friday and I have to have the car." The reply most likely will be, "You don't have to have the car," or "You don't have to date every Friday night," or "You don't have to have a car to have a date." Regardless of the reply, what really caused it, was the "non-listening" climate Bill established. The overtones of Bill's message is "I'm demanding the car; I don't give a darn what you think; I'm the one that counts and I'm going to get the car." Bill actually placed a barrier between himself and his father.

Bill's initial remarks seemed selfish to his father. The fact that Bill didn't mean to be selfish, doesn't matter. The way he came across to his father is what determined the father's receptivity and established the climate. So in effect, Bill's initial statement was: "Here's the kind of discussions we're going to have Dad, we're going to have an argument over the car." Bill established a "non-listening" climate.

Now let's look at an example of the same situation, with one difference. This time Bill intends to make sure that his father will be receptive, will listen open-mindedly to what he has to say. This time Bill will try to establish a good listening climate for communications between himself and his father.

"Dad, I would like to talk to you about using the car. How do you feel about me using the family car for a date?" This time the climate is entirely different. Bill has said, in effect: "I'd like to use the car, but I'm not trying to be selfish. I'm interested in your feelings, in your opinions. I'd like to discuss it with you." He has established a listening climate. Bill still may not get the car, but if he doesn't, the refusal will come after discussion rather than argument. He won't be turned down simply because of a non-listening" climate, like the one he created in the first example.

Any time that we establish a "non-listening" climate, we eliminate any chance we might have of getting our point across to the other person. We lose the opportunity to get him to weigh our arguments logically. He can't look at the evidence we present if he feels challenged to a "duel" of words.

How a Non-Listening Climate Is Established

Starting an argument is only one of many ways to establish a "non-listening" climate. You can do it by not listening to the other person, by interrupting him before he has completely finished expressing his thoughts, by ignoring what he says, by overwhelming him, by pressuring him, by trying to manipulate, exploit, or take advantage, by high pressuring, or by many other selfish behaviors.

In all of these examples, you are saying to the other person: "You are unimportant, I am the one that counts here, and this is how our discussion is going to go. I'll talk and you listen. If you try to say something, I'll interrupt you. If you do manage to get something said, I'll ignore it. So why don't you just "shut up" and accept everything I say as gospel."

It is easy to understand that, under those circumstances, the other party will not be inclined to listen. To look at another example of "non-listening," as a result of creating a "non-listening" climate, let's assume that Bill and his father have a new problem. During the previous discussion, the second example, Bill agreed to keep his grades up, in school, in return for the privilege of using the car each Thursday night.

In the past Bill has always received"A's" and "B's" in school. This time, after having the car for a month, Bill received a "C" in one of his classes. Bill's father is now contemplating taking the car away from Bill. He feels that Bill has not lived up to the agreement and the penalty should be the loss of the car.

The father's real purpose is to get Bill to keep his grades up. He also wishes to use this situation to explain to Bill the seriousness of living up to an agreement. Keeping an agreement, he feels, is one of the few ways a young person has to demonstrate his integrity.

Bill's father must develop a listening climate, if he wishes Bill to be attentive to his words, to weigh the reasons and evidence he presents, and to understand the importance of keeping his agreements as a matter of integrity. If the father does not develop a listening climate, he will fail. He will not get his message accepted in a "non-listening" climate. Bill's father now begins the conversation.

"Bill, as soon as you felt your grades slipping, you should have come to me and relinquished your car privileges. You should have told me that you were unable to keep your grades up and were turning in your car key in order not to break your agreement. That would have shown your integrity and would have kept me from the unpleasant chore of taking the car away from you."

In spite of the father's good intentions, he has created a "non-listening" climate. The message coming across to Bill is "You knew your grades were dropping and kept it hid or lied about it. Your word is no good; you have no integrity and can't be trusted." Bill's reaction to this may be anxiety or anger. Whichever emotional state Bill's reaction falls in, it will be one in which he will not listen. He may just tune out or he may retort in anger. He may respond with "You'll enjoy taking the car away from me." The argument has begun, no listening occurs, and no learning or understanding takes place.

How Bill's Father Established a Listening Climate

The way for the father to create a listening climate is to check out Bill's feelings. Just as Bill showed an interest in his father's feelings when asking for car privileges, the father can create a listening climate by showing an interest in Bill's feelings. To demonstrate the correct way, we start the example with Bill's father speaking.

"Bill, I'm concerned about the 'C' on your report card. How do you feel about it?" In this example Bill doesn't feel threatened by his father. The message from Bill's father is: "I'm interested in how you feel, what your opinion is." Bill is not, as a result of his father's initial remarks, going to become anxious or angry. His mind will not be closed off, he can listen to his father. He knows his father is concerned about the "C" and he knows he has an agreement to keep his grades up.

As the conversation develops, some important points may come out. Bill's father has no way to get these points out, except by asking Bill. For example, the "C" might be a mistake. I know of a number of instances where "C's" were recorded in error, when the student had earned a "B". Another point is that Bill may think getting a "C" is keeping his grades up. "C" is an average grade and may be satisfactory as far as Bill is concerned.

The important point is that by letting Bill relate his feelings, tell his story, say what he thinks, Bill will be receptive to what his father says. Since the father listened to Bill, Bill will listen to the father.

The principle of checking the other person's feelings to create a listening climate is not just a family situation. It works in any interaction between any two people.

HOW TO MOTIVATE PEOPLE TO SUPPORT YOUR IDEAS AND PLANS

It is generally agreed among psychologists and educators that you cannot motivate people to do what you want them to do. Although most people would argue that you can influence people's behavior, they admit that motivation results from internal desires to fulfill personal needs.

For the purposes of clarification, we distinguish between motivation and behavior, with behavior being an action caused by an individual's motivation. Motivation then is an internal force developed from an internal tension, resulting from a desire to gain satisfaction. This motivation causes behavior that is determined by individual expectations, utilizing behavior that the individual believes will be successful.

In order to get people to support your ideas and plans, you must tie in to their motivation. Connect your ideas and plans to their needs, desires, or expectations. If you try to persuade someone to taste salt when he has been without water for two or three days, your efforts to persuade will fail. If, on the other hand, you try to persuade him to eat an apple, your chances are greatly improved. Here then is the secret of getting your point of view accepted. Tie your persuasive efforts in to helping the other person fulfill his or her needs. If you can determine the motivating need and relate to that need, your chances of success are greatly enhanced.

If you ignore the motivating need, you won't even get the other person's attention. While his mind is preoccupied with thoughts of how to get water, he won't hear what you say about other subjects. Only those messages that he interprets as leading to the fulfillment of his need are likely to register.

The best chance then of getting the other person to listen is to tie in to some need that person has. If your message can be related to that need, you should show that relationship in your conversation. Then he will listen to you.

Handling Interference Caused by Unconscious Needs

We are not always consciously aware of our needs. For some long forgotten reason we may have suppressed a desire to be recognized as a leader, a skilled worker, or an authority on some subject. Since the desire is there, though hidden from consciousness, we are subconsciously driven to acquire and demonstrate the skills leading to the recognition we desire.

Often these unconscious or hidden motivations interfere with our conversations. In an effort to satisfy our need for recognition, we interject praise of ourselves. Depending upon our social and verbal skills, we may subtly praise ourselves, or we may obnoxiously claim great achievements and glory.

Learn to accept these interferences. Since they are unconscious, they are not something to blame or criticize the other person for. Recognize them as clues that an unconscious need of the other party is not being fulfilled. Then help the other person fulfill those needs and win his support for your own plans and ideas.

If you see that the need is for recognition, look for some skill or knowledge that the person has that deserves praise. Then offer sincere praise, recognition, or reassurance. When you understand his needs, you also can better relate your point of view to the thinking of the other person.

Don't be discouraged if he continues to seek recognition time after time. Even though you may have given him recognition and reassurance over a long period of time, he may seek more. He may have felt deprived of recognition for years, so he won't get over it in a short period of time.

When he consciously and unconsciously develops a new self-image—an image of a person who is properly recognized for his knowledge and skills—his recognition-seeking behavior will subside.

How to Determine People's Motivations

You can best get your message across by finding something in your point of view that will benefit the other person. In order to determine that benefit, analyze him to see what his needs are. Think back to the things he has said in the past, and determine what need was being expressed.

Suppose you remember that he has often spoken of trying new things, of making experiments, of seeking new achievements. You can relate those statements to Maslow's model of basic human needs. Seeking new things and new achievements all fall in Maslow's self-actualization category. You then know that your acquaintance has a need to satisfy his motivation for self-actualization. If there is anything new, experimental, or challenging about your idea, make it known. This knowledge can be an influencing factor on the self-actualizing person. The easiest way to persuade is to find a benefit to satisfy the needs the other person is already motivated to fulfill.

Suppose your conversational partner's needs are for esteem; he is motivated to seek expressions of praise or recognition from other people. In his conversations he will make statements that describe his power, independence, wisdom, ability, and accomplishments. To get your idea across to this person, let the idea become his. Question what he thinks about each point until he accepts the idea as his own. If the idea will enhance his status, prestige, recognition or power, you will have helped him satisfy his need for esteem.

A person who is primarily motivated by social needs, talks about his needs. He speaks of the joy of friendship or his desire to spend more time with people. Since he likes people, he has a tendency to describe everyone in glowing terms. He sees the best in people and makes excuses for their shortcomings. Being primarily motivated by social needs, he needs to talk. He talks about social and sports events. One of the clues that he is socially motivated is that he talks a lot. If you can relate your idea in terms that provide a satisfaction of this person's social needs, he will be more likely to accept the idea. If he can see its social significance, he will tend to commit himself to the idea and support it.

The person who is primarily motivated by security needs will express fear of any situation that is different. If he has not had experience with an idea or situation, he will fear that its consequences will affect him adversely. In his mind the best thing to do is to stick with the familiar. The familiar he can trust. The best way to get your idea across to a security-oriented person is to make it familiar. Take each part of the idea and relate it to something he is already familiar with.

Personal trust is very important in dealing with the security-oriented person. If he has extremely high trust in you, he will trust your idea, if you present it in a non-threatening way.

Biological needs, the need for food, air, water, and rest and relaxation are easily determined. These life-preserving needs are quickly and easily satisfied. The mind recognizes the benefit of putting away some of the necessities for future use. You can relate your ideas to future needs and thus help satisfy the biological needs.

Just as a reminder, we all have some needs from all the motivating need categories. These needs change from time to time. We should be prepared to change our presentation to relate to the particular need being expressed at any one time.

How Self-Image Relates to Idea Acceptance

One reason a person rejects certain attitudes is his belief that the attitude is not consistent with his self-image. He will be more likely accept an attitude, idea, or persuasion that is consistent with his self-image.

If a person holds an image of himself as an aggressive, pushy, self-centered person, he will accept arguments that the rest of the world is the same way. He will accept as "true" arguments that it's a "dog-eat-dog" world. Statements that "everyone is out to get what they can" are interpreted by him to mean "out to take advantage of others." All arguments that portray people as being hostile or selfish will be readily accepted by the person who holds a hostile self-image.

One with the hostile self-image will attribute the kind acts of others to some hidden motive. Since people often have multiple motives for doing things, he can usually find some motive to support his belief. In a situation where he sees someone make a large donation to a charitable organization, he will credit the contributions as being due to the tax motive. He will overlook the fact that only a portion of the contribution will be saved in actual tax reduction.

If a person holds a charitable, warm hearted image of himself, he will be easily persuaded to accept arguments that are consistent with that image. This person also believes the rest of the world to be the same as himself. He recognizes, as does our hostile friend, that there are a few different from himself, but believes them to be very few in number.

Since people generally see themselves as being similar to most people, you can gain some insight into their self-image by listening to what they say about others. As they describe others, they describe themselves. A man who says "all men are thieves," sees himself as being a thief. The exception to this rule is when he makes prejudiced statements about a specific race or class of people other than his own race or group. The fact that he separates himself from the group described indicates that he holds a self-image that differs from the trait he ascribed to the group.

People also give us clues to their self-image in describing their own goals and aspirations. A person who talks about becoming a doctor in order to help people is describing a "help others" self-image. A person who talks about working himself up the ladder in a corporation may see himself as having a "help others" self-image. The things he describes himself doing as a corporate executive will give further clues to his self-image.

Once you understand the person's self-image, you can avoid using arguments that conflict with his self-image. The self-image is a truth to the individual. Anything that is consistent with the attitudes and beliefs making up the self-image can be accepted as true. Any idea or statement that is inconsistent with the self-image may be considered untrue.

Now you have some understanding of the magnitude of the task you have in getting your idea accepted. If that idea is inconsistent with any of the factors making up the self-image, you face an almost impregnable obstacle. If the idea is worthy of the effort required in this circumstance, be aware that what you are attempting is to change the other person's self-concept.

One method of persuading someone to accept an idea that seems inconsistent with his self-image is to show him that some of his beliefs are inconsistent with some of his other strongly held beliefs (discussed previously).

People also develop habits that preserve their self-image. They develop the habit of arguing against certain ideas. Or they develop the habit of automatically accepting information that is favorable to certain ideas that are consistent with their self-image.

If you can get the other person to change some of the protective habits he has developed, you may get him to see the logic of your viewpoint. If he automatically rejects certain arguments, avoid making flat assertions concerning those arguments. Secure his participation in exploring the evidence you used in building the argument.

By exploring the evidence together, you have an opportunity to discuss the various possible results of the evidence. Take one point at a time to try to reach an agreement on small segments without using the entire argument, which would challenge his self-concept.

By looking at the evidence in this manner, the other person learns to see both sides of the story. He begins to see that he can explore various points of view without endangering himself. He, over a period of time, begins to change the old habit. When the new habit is formed—exploring all ideas—he has changed his self-image.

You can't always change the other person's mind, but you can at least be aware of the reason he is resisting your idea. Avoid making statements that you know will challenge his self-image. Also be flexible enough to change your own opinion, when the other person's logic shows you to be wrong. One of the best ways to influence others is by example. If you openly admit errors and show your willingness to change your mind, it will catch on. The other person will be willing to do the same.

How Joan Summers Used Conversational Magic to Win Financial Backing

Joan Summers, after tens years experience as a public relations manager, decided to go into business for herself. She had saved enough money to live for one year but needed money to operate the office. She decided to approach the local bank and ask for a six month loan to run the office.

Joan confronted a stuffy loan manager who obviously wanted recognition for his position and his experience. Joan asked for the loan officer's opinions that she might have the benefit of his experience. He responded with information about both successful and unsuccessful business attempts. From this conversation, Joan learned the problems the loan officer feared and also learned that he held a self-image as a helpful community leader.

Joan used the information from that conversation to win support for her loan. She overcame the loan officer's fears by pointing out that, by the end of a six month period, she would have earned enough to repay the loan, or she would use her living expense money to repay the loan and go back to work for another company. Either way the bank would recover the loan.

Finally, she expressed her admiration for the loan officer's interest and support of local business people, especially those who were just starting and needed the advice of an established member of the financial community. She again assured him of her ability to repay the loan. She got the loan and established her public relations business; the bank became one of her first customers.

12

Conversational Techniques That Create Psychological Obligations

There are a few people who are so self-centered that they never listen. They are so preoccupied with their own thoughts and plans that they block out and refuse to listen to other people's ideas. These people also become emotionally involved with ideas or plans of action and refuse to compromise or evaluate ideas of others. As difficult as they are to deal with, they *can* be convinced to listen.

In this chapter, you'll learn ways to develop psychological obligations. You'll see how to get people to listen to your ideas and learn ways to get them to evaluate what you say open-mindedly. Finally, in this chapter, techniques are revealed that develop psychological obligations to compromise. With these techniques you can become a master conversationalist.

HOW TO DEVELOP A PSYCHOLOGICAL OBLIGATION FOR A PERSON TO LISTEN TO YOU

A method that psychologists used in counseling disturbed patients has been adapted for use in conversation. This technique encompasses four areas that establish trust and build an obligation on the part of the other person to listen to you. The four areas are:

1. Respond to the Other Person's Feelings
2. Protect the Other Person's Pride
3. Don't Be a Bearer of Gloom
4. Show That You Are Listening

Respond to the Other Person's Feelings

The most important area in building a psychological obligation is the other person's feelings. Time after time, when investigating complaints made by employees in industrial organizations, we heard, "They don't care what happens to us." The employees felt that their supervisors had ignored their complaints because the supervisors didn't care, rather than the complaints not being warranted. We trained the supervisors to respond to the employees' feelings by "mirroring" and summarizing the employees' statements.

Mirroring a statement is repeating it back to the other person without comment. This shows the employee that you are interested in what he or she has to say. Summarizing is simply repeating what the other person says in your own words. Summarizing shows that you are listening and trying to understand.

For example, in one situation, a supervisor who had been trained in these techniques interviewed an employee who had been constantly complaining. During the interview, the employee said, "Everyone ignores my complaints." The supervisor mirrored back the complaint, "You feel that everyone ignores your complaints?" The employee replied, "Yes, no one tried to see how these new policies affect my work." The supervisor summarized, "You feel your complaints are being ignored because no one looks at the effect on your work?"

As the supervisor continued to respond to the employee's feelings, the employee began to see that this supervisor did care. The employee pointed out where real problems existed and backed off where his complaints weren't legitimate.

Protect the Other Person's Pride

Even when people are wrong, they need to retain their pride. If you want someone to listen to you, you must be very careful not to do anything to take his pride away. If you must correct an individual, either do it privately or leave the corrected person an out. For example, you might first give some additional information and use that information to explain why the corrected person was in error. He couldn't have been in error if he had previously been aware of the new information.

Always be alert to the feelings of pride that people have. Don't make them feel a loss of pride. Rather than criticizing people, relate your remarks to incidents or situations. If people learn that they can trust you not to criticize or belittle them, they will respect you, speak freely and feel an obligation to listen when you speak.

Don't Be a Bearer of Gloom

People avoid those who consistently complain or often tell stories of hardship or gloom. Most people have enough problems of their own without listening to someone else's all the time. If you persist in carrying stories of gloom, they will build an adversive reaction to you and will avoid contact with you whenever possible.

If you want people to look forward to talking to you, speak of happy things. Be optimistic and cheerful, and they will look forward to listening to you. This doesn't mean that you can't share your burdens with close friends and family members. We all need to talk out our problems but the point is don't dwell on them. Talk them out and move on to happier things.

Show That You Are Listening

To build a psychological obligation for the other person to listen to you, you must show him that *you* are listening. Make comments that show that you have been, are, and will continue to listen. Do this by making neutral comments, asking questions, summarizing, and responding to emotion.

Neutral comments. A neutral comment is a statement that neither approves nor disapproves the ideas being presented. Neutral comments are generally short. For example, "I see what your point is," or "I understand what you're trying to describe." Also, "I see," "Uh huh," or "Keep going" are neutral comments. A neutral comment doesn't necessarily mean you agree, it simply shows that you are listening and paying attention. It creates the climate that leads to the build-up of a psychological obligation to listen.

Asking questions. You can also show you are listening by asking questions. If you relate each question to a specific point made by the other person, you prove without doubt that you are listening. You, obviously, can't ask questions if you aren't listening. If you are listening, but can't think of a question, you may think of one that begins with, how, when, where, why, what or who. Asking these questions will give you a better understanding of the other person's point of view and show that you are listening.

Summarizing. Another way to show that you are listening is by summarizing what the other person said. If you have missed a point or misunderstood something, your summary provides an opportunity to correct any misunderstanding. Ask the other person if your summary is a correct restatement of what has been said. If it is incorrect, he can correct it. Again you show that you are listening, and you continue to build an obligation for the other person to listen to you.

Responding to emotions. The final courtesy that you can perform is to respond to the emotional expressions of the other person. This is probably the most effective of the four courteous methods that you can use in building an obligation to listen. If you respond to his emotions he appreciates your personal concern and feels obligated to show a similar courtesy to you.

In summary, by making neutral comments, asking questions, summarizing, and responding to emotion, you display courtesy, respect, interest, attention, and human understanding. Although you may occasionally encounter someone who will not respond to courteous treatment, generally, you will find that these courtesies will build an obligation for the other person to listen to you.

How Bob Johnson Developed a Psychological Obligation and Won a New Friend

Bob Johnson had just arrived in town and had found a job in a department store. He had not had time to make new friends but knew that you don't make friends by forcing friendship. Bob had read that friendships form on the basis of sharing feelings, problems, and fears and a willingness to listen to others.

A few days later, one of the saleswomen in the store told Bob that she was upset because she could not get Saturday off. She had made plans for the weekend and now everything would have to be called off.

Bob expressed understanding by responding to her emotion. He said he agreed that working Saturday would foul up the weekend. He told her he could understand her feelings. He listened, used neutral comments, asked questions, summarized, and responded to emotions. Later Bob talked to her about his own problems. She felt obligated to listen. Soon the two began to talk every day and became close friends. Bob's use of conversational magic not only developed an obligation for another person to listen, but also won a new friend.

CONVERSATIONAL TECHNIQUES THAT OBLIGATE PEOPLE TO EVALUATE YOUR IDEAS OPEN-MINDEDLY

To develop an obligation for another person to open-mindedly evaluate your ideas, *avoid conversational irritants* that cause people to tune you out. Also *develop persuasive techniques* that obligate your listener to be open-minded.

Avoid Conversational Irritants

Many people, who are otherwise good conversationalists, lose their listeners because of irritating conversational habits.

The most irritating of these habits are making egotistical remarks, belittling another's point of view, counterarguing, and refusing to listen to new information.

Making egotistical remarks. The quickest and most certain way to irritate your listener is to give the impression that you are a know-it-all. If you take a position that you personally have all the answers, that whatever you say is non-negotiable, and that your remarks are final, you will irritate your listener and cut off any possibility of developing an obligation for your listener to evaluate your ideas.

Belittling other people's views. Another way to irritate others is to belittle their remarks or comments. As a matter of fact, anything that makes the other person feel you are putting him or her down will result in resentment and a refusal to evaluate your ideas. When an individual feels he is being put down, he becomes emotionally distressed and rejects logic. He will not attempt to open-mindedly evaluate your ideas.

Counterarguing. If you offer any argument whatsoever in opposition to what the other person is saying, you are setting a stage for him to do the same when you try to make your point. Rather than counterargue, try to understand the other person's point of view. If you ask questions and seek understanding, he will tend to do the same later when you give your opinion. So, no matter how much you oppose the view being expressed, don't counterargue if you want that person to later evaluate your point of view open-mindedly.

Refusing to listen. Have you ever become so distressed with what the other person is saying that you just stopped listening? In some cases a person has become so distressed that he actually told the other person that he would not listen any longer. This behavior reflects an attitude that there is not even a small segment of logic or reason in the statements being made. That attitude obviously leads to problems. If only by accident, there could be at least one logical comment made by the other person.

Even if there is no valuable comment or logical statement made by the other person, the refusal to listen cuts off any possibility of correcting that person's thinking. Listening, without criticism, has been shown to help a person clarify his thoughts. In any event, you must listen in order to build the obligation for the other person to return the favor. If you want your ideas evaluated, you must have someone listen to them.

Develop Persuasive Techniques

Research has shown that certain behaviors, certain conversational techniques can generate a psychological obligation on the part of the person you are conversing with. These techniques are behavioral in nature because they relate more to how we speak than what we say. The following persuasive techniques are drawn from a number of research projects and have been proven effective in both industrial and social situations. The techniques are to evaluate the other person's ideas, cite experts or well-known people to support your ideas, point out the adverse consequences of not utilizing your ideas, speak with conviction, and avoid pressure tactics.

Evaluate the other person's ideas. To show an individual that you are open-mindedly evaluating his ideas, ask questions. Ask for comparisons of his ideas with other similar and dissimilar concepts. Ask how the idea will work in various situations. Make comments such as, "I wonder how your idea could be applied to a situation where . . ." Questions and comments that show you are evaluating his ideas will encourage him to show you the same courtesy.

Cite experts to support your ideas. If there are important people or experts who support your point of view, cite them. People have been shown to value and assume the ideas of important political, social, and industrial people. They believe these people have studied the issues and have come to logical conclusions.

Point out the adverse consequences of not utilizing your idea. If an idea is good, there should be good consequences of utilizing the idea. In addition to mentioning these good consequences or benefits, you should also point out the adverse consequences of your idea not being accepted. It is important, however, not to overdo the negative aspects of rejection. Studies have shown that mild negative appeals are much more effective

than strong negative appeals. Evidently strong negative appeals
are seen as a form of manipulation.

Speak with conviction. If a person is to be persuaded to accept your point of view, he must be sure that you are truly
convinced of the position you take. Since many people repeat
ideas they are not sure of, you must speak with conviction and
sincerity. So, speak firmly and with emphasis on key words. Do
not express emotion or anger, simply express your ideas firmly to
show conviction.

Avoid pressure tactics. Never use pressure or manipulation
to force your point of view. An idea or point of view must withstand the onslaught of conflicting ideas over a period of time. A
forced idea or opinion is good only as long as the presence of the
force is hovering over the person the idea is forced upon.

A better persuasive technique is one that establishes a belief
in the idea that will withstand argument. The person holding the
idea should be able to evaluate it against opposing ideas, test it
against specific challenges, and support it with logic and reason.

By following the persuasive techniques described in this
chapter, you will be able to develop a psychological obligation
for people to listen to your opinions, evaluate your ideas, and
support you in actions you wish to take to get your ideas
established.

How Cliff Johnson Created
a Psychological Obligation
That Saved His Job

Cliff Johnson was called in by his production foreman and
was told that business was bad and that he was being laid off in-
definitely. Cliff asked the foreman, "Just how bad are things?"
The foreman told Cliff that productivity was down and that it
was difficult to compete with companies that produced lower
costs goods.

Cliff suspected that the productivity issue related to him
personally. He asked the foreman a question to determine if his
own productivity was low and to show that he was listening.
Cliff's suspicion was confirmed. The foreman revealed that his
records showed Cliff's productivity to be the lowest in the
department.

Cliff did not argue, he made neutral comments, he summarized, he responded to emotional statements with concern. He slowly built an obligation for the foreman to listen to his story. When Cliff saw that the foreman was willing to listen, he told his story. Cliff pointed out that his machinery had been broken down an average of two hours per day for the last two weeks.

Cliff spoke with conviction about his level of production during the time his machinery was operating properly. He did not try to pressure the foreman into putting him back to work. However, Cliff mentioned one or two of the highest producers who had seen the breakdown, and how they had commented on his loss of productivity due to the breakdown. Finally, the foreman suggested that Cliff remain at work, and he, the foreman, would study the problem. By developing an obligation for the foreman to listen, Cliff retained his job.

HOW TO BUILD AN OBLIGATION
FOR YOUR LISTENER TO COMPROMISE

To build an obligation for your listener to compromise, you must express high ideals. Show that you are willing to compromise and that your objectives are worthy of compromise.

State a worthy objective. In order to get an individual to relax his position and make compromises, you must give him a reason to do so. If you can show that you have an objective that is worthwhile, you can create an obligation for compromise. The other person will be drawn to this worthwhile idea and feel an obligation to compromise. To fail to compromise would leave the other person feeling guilty for refusing to support something that is worthwhile.

Express high ideals. Everyone is attracted to high ideals. The secret of the world's greatest leaders is that they all expressed high ideals. A friend of mine used to say that he had an obligation to his ancestors. "They were of low bloodlines but high ideals," he said. All of them lived by those high ideals regardless of their station in life. Their motto was, "Whatever trade or profession you choose, become the very best."

In order to build an obligation to compromise, express your position in terms of some high ideal. Once the ideal is expressed by you, and understood by the other person, the obligation is established. If compromise is required, it is much easier to justify when the compromise is toward higher ideals.

Demonstrate your willingness to compromise. A demonstration of your willingness to compromise is the good faith action that convinces the other person that you are fair and creates an obligation for him to compromise also. Select a number of minor points that do not undermine your main objective, compromise on those small points, and the other person will feel obligated to compromise to show that he is as reasonable as you are.

A retired psychologist, whom I knew, pretends that he retired broke because he did not learn to compromise in time to save his business. He tells the following story on himself, which he says was his last case.

> A man came to see me, not to seek my advice but to get his wife off his back. His wife had complained about his obnoxious behavior until he finally agreed to see me. He was bitter and angry with his wife and took his hostility out on me. He argued with me for over an hour and I decided I could not help him.
>
> I told him that he was dismissed and suggested that he not come back. In an apparent change of heart, he calmly said, "What did you find?" I answered, "You're crazy!" He retorted, "I want another opinion." I said, "O.K., you're an ugly patient, that's another opinion."

My friend laughingly says his own unwillingness to compromise cost him his practice. Whether he is serious or not is not really important. The important point to remember is that compromise leads to compromise and argument leads to counterargument.

Express understanding. One of the most powerful techniques for developing an obligations to compromise is to express understanding. When you carefully question the other person, gain understanding, and then express your understanding for his point of view, the other person feels obligated to show you the same courtesy. The understanding gained leads to compromise on both sides. You can develop an obligation for the people you deal with, to compromise by expressing your understanding of his point of view.

How Ellen Smith's Compromise Resulted in a Raise

Ellen Smith, a secretary, worked for three people. She handled all the correspondence, filing and phone calls for all three. The work load was heavy when all three were in town, but was relatively light when one of the three was out of town. Ellen worked hard and put in extra time when all three were at work and relaxed, as she felt she was entitled to, when one of the three was out of town.

A new manager was hired and Ellen was asked to handle the secretarial duties for the new manager. Ellen's first reaction was that she could not handle any additional work. Her supervisor reminded her that when one of her managers was out of town, she did not have enough to do.

Ellen used the techniques listed in this chapter to build an obligation for her supervisor to compromise. Ellen, first, stated that she wanted to continue to do superior work and did not want to take on so much work that the quality of her work would be affected.

After expressing the worthy objection—maintaining high quality work—Ellen then demonstrated her own willingness to compromise. She suggested that if the workload could be leveled out on the days when all the managers were in town, she would be able to do the work for the new manager.

Ellen then expressed her understanding of the problem. She said she knew there was not enough work to hire an additional secretary and would do whatever she could to help solve the problem. Ellen's supervisor also compromised. She assigned Ellen to the new manager, but arranged for Ellen to transfer her overflow to another department on the days that all four of her managers were in the office. She also gave Ellen a raise which she said that Ellen deserved for the additional work and her attitude in solving the problem.

13

Persuasion:
The Key to Conversational Magic

The greatest magic in conversation is the magic of persuasion. To be able to influence someone else to see your point of view or accept your opinion is the ultimate use of psychological persuasion. By learning the techniques presented here, you can improve your relations with other people, advance in your chosen area, and improve your general well being.

In this chapter, you will learn the techniques developed by psychologists, educators, and communications specialists. You will learn to use the persuasion process to get people to see things from your point of view. You'll read examples of people using this process to get specific results at home, at work, and in social situations. You'll see how to use the conversational magic of persuasion to get commitment to the things you want done.

THE PERSUASION PROCESS

Elements of the persuasion process are related below in a step-by-step sequence. Follow this sequence in order, except step numbers 6, 7, and 8 which are responses to the other person's statements. Use them when appropriate to deal effectively with resistance. The ten steps of persuasion are:

1. Develop a Favorable Climate
2. Direct Attention to Your Topic
3. Select the Proper Time
4. State Your Conclusion
5. Focus on the Problem
6. Restate the Other Person's Response
7. Mirror Back Emotional Responses
8. Clarify Resistance
9. Use Constructive Questioning
10. Summarize Your Evidence and Conclusions

Develop a Favorable Climate

One principle of understanding is that the other person must be in a state of readiness. In other words, he or she must be inclined to listen to what you have to say. You can't persuade someone to do something or accept what you say if he isn't willing to listen. This readiness to listen can be developed by creating a favorable listening climate, one that is open, supportive, and free of criticism. This climate must be maintained throughout the discussion. If you establish clearly that you will not criticize, the other person will be more likely to be free and open and be willing to listen to what you say.

Rather than criticizing, belittling, or taking exception with what others say, seek understanding. If you take exception, for example, the other person may "dig in" and become protective of his or her position. He then becomes more fully committed to his own position and will be less willing to evaluate what you say.

You can develop a favorable climate by speaking softly, acting as though acceptance of your idea is not vitally important to you, and showing that you are willing to listen to the ideas expressed by the other person. All of these things take pressure from the situation and establish friendliness which is the key to creating a favorable climate.

Direct Attention to Your Topic

Often someone is distracted by his own thoughts or other activities. In order to persuade, you must get him to direct his attention to the topic you wish to discuss. There are a number of ways to get a person's attention, but the following are the most productive and logical. The factors most likely to succeed in gaining attention are *Intensity, Contrast, Movement, Repetition,* and *Novelty.*

Intensity. Build intensity into your comments by using your voice and facial expressions in the examples you give. Intensify words by speaking them in crisp, distinct syllables, by chopping them off sharply, and by raising your voice slightly. Use facial expressions to intensify your message by looking solemn or stern.

Intensity is also produced in conversation by the use of concrete rather than abstract words and phrases. Concrete words evoke mental images which catch and hold attention. For example, the word "rocking chair" evokes a more specific image than the word chair. "Be at work by 8 a.m." is more concrete than "Go to work," or "Win $50,000" is more specific than "Win a contest." By using specific concrete examples, you will more easily catch and hold the attention of others.

Contrast. Again, to get attention you may use contrast. Contrast aimed at any of the sense will be effective. Contrast size, sound, color, texture, taste, or smell. Gain attention by describing or demonstrating the contrast of whatever differences occur.

Movement. Everyone is familiar with the reaction we all have to movement. Our curiosity causes us to examine the movement to see what change is taking place. Any change interests us, so you can use change or movement to capture the attention of others. The movement can be gestures or it can be a verbal description of some change your idea will effect.

Repetition. In addition to catching attention, repetition can bore and turn people off. So, to avoid boring your audience, don't repeat the same sentence twice. You may repeat the idea, however, by saying it in a different way. Use a different function or discuss a different application of the idea. All of these methods will give you repetition that will catch and hold attention.

Novelty. Novelty is characterized by the unexpected or unusual. If you can find an unusual way to present your idea, you will get attention. Don't "go overboard," however, and become so outlandish that the novelty becomes the main attraction. For example, humor is often used to create novelty. If the joke is so new and novel that it takes the spotlight rather than support your point of view, you may gain attention but not benefit from it.

Select the Propert Time

Timing is the most important step in the persuasive process. If you present your idea at the wrong time, you may not even be heard. When people are emotionally distressed, preoccupied with distracting thoughts or preconceived ideas, the time is wrong. Most people know this but don't know how to handle it.

The secret is to be supportive and work toward developing the proper timing. First, recognize that when an individual becomes defensive, argumentative, overbearing, or secretive, he is acting out a motivational drive and usually is not aware of it. To satisfy the drive, you simply relate in a supportive way to the feeling or emotion being expressed.

If a person reveals anger by becoming argumentative, don't argue. Deal with the anger. Say, "I believe you are mad. Tell me what happened." Then express understanding for that anger. Say, "I can see that you would be angry under those conditions." If the person you are talking to keeps looking away or seems unusually quiet, indicating he is preoccupied, then you simply say, "You seem to be preoccupied. Is something bothering you?"

By asking these questions and showing understanding, you help your companion finish or work out the anger or preoccupations. Once this occurs, you will have developed the right timing. The other person will show that your timing is right by asking you questions, by evaluating your suggestions, or by showing approval for some part of what you have said. When any of these comments occur, you will know that your timing is right.

State Your Conclusion

If you are presenting evidence that builds to a conclusion, you will have a greater chance of your idea being accepted if you specifically state your conclusion. Research has shown that people frequently jump to the wrong conclusion. Because of previously held convictions, they listen to the portion of your comments that seem to support their own beliefs.

When your comments are not in accordance with someone's previously held convictions or do not support his attitudes and beliefs, the person tends to glaze over or only half hear them. If you state your conclusion, the statements that are usually seen as unimportant are then seen as support for the conclusion you have given. With an understanding that these comments are meant to support specific conclusions, the person will listen more carefully.

Finally, with your conclusion clearly stated, the listener cannot use your statements as a "ladder" to reach his or her own conclusions. If he rejects your conclusion, he must develop evidence to support his own conclusions.

Focus on the Problem

Often someone will introduce extraneous material. He will argue against your principles in order to support some pet project of his own. By winning an argument to support some pet project, he will believe that in the process he has proven your point wrong. The best way to deal with such a person is to keep him focused on the problem or idea that you are trying to promote. If he begins to stray from the topic you are discussing, politely draw him back on the track.

To keep him on the problem, ask questions or make comments that bring him back to the point or discussion you are concerned with. When an extraneous subject comes up, simply say, "That's interesting, but we need to settle my topic before starting something else." Or, after the new topic has been discussed for one or two minutes, say, "I can see you have an important subject which will take quite a bit of time. Let's get subject "A" finished, and then we'll tackle your topic."

Restate the Other Person's Response

One of the most valuable techniques in the persuasion process is to restate the responses or statements made by the other person. This will cause him to think about, evaluate, and possibly change his or her opinion. When someone hears his idea expressed by someone else, he hears it as it sounds rather than as he intended to say it. He is freed from his own biased intentions and can evaluate what someone else says. This often results in a more rational evaluation and a change in opinion toward the position you hold.

It is much easier, psychologically, for a person to say that you have misinterpreted what he said than it is for him to say that he is wrong. So, by repeating back his comments, you give him an opportunity to change his opinion.

You may repeat the entire sentence just as he spoke it or rephrase what he said in terms that convey the message you understood him to be trying to get across. In either case you are providing the person an opportunity to change. If you don't get any change in his second response and you still feel he is wrong, then apply his opinion to a specific example. You might say, "If I understand your opinion correctly, we could apply it to the housing industry by temporarily building tents in the desert. This would hold costs to an absolute minimum in line with your opinion as I understand it."

You may also just repeat the key words or the last three or four words the other person says. This will show you are evaluating and will cause him to think carefully and chose words that more clearly explain his point of view. By restating, whether a few words, a sentence or an idea, you give the other person an opportunity to reflect and change his or her opinion.

Mirror Back Emotional Responses

Emotional responses block understanding and must be cleared away as part of the persuasion process. If a person becomes fearful, happy, sad or frustrated, these emotional reactions are more powerful motivations than the motivation to listen or try to understand. In order to get your point of view understood, you must first deal with these emotions.

The way to deal with an emotion is to ventilate it—draw it out. Get the other person to focus on the emotion, express it, and work it out. You do this by mirroring back the emotion. This process is similar to using a two-way mirror. You reflect back the emotion but let the message go through.

If someone is really joyful, he might say, "I just got promoted and I'm really happy about it." When you respond— to reflect the emotion—you say, "I can see you are really happy." By talking only about the happy feeling, you focus the other person's attention to the emotion. The person will continue to talk about how happy he or she is until the emotion is fully ventilated.

Use the same process to deal with any kind of emotion that is expressed. If someone indicates that he is sad, say, "You seem to be sad today." If he expresses fear, say, "You act as though you are afraid." If he shows despair, you might say, "You seem to be disillusioned." If he shows frustration, say, "You seem to be upset."

In all of these situations, the person is directed to the emotion. As he expresses the emotion and talks about the underlying cause, he begins to clear his own mind. The person ventilates the emotion and sees his problems more clearly. He begins to find solutions and form rational plans to deal with the problems. As he becomes more rational, he is more willing to listen and try to understand your point of view.

Clarify Resistance

In every conversation, in every persuasive effort, we will encounter some resistance. Our first reaction to resistance is usually to try to overcome the resistance with pressure or counterargument. We somehow believe that if we argue long enough or loud enough or use enough pressure that we can overwhelm the other person and change his or her mind. This, of course, is not true. We can overwhelm people and get them to "clam up" perhaps, but we cannot persuade them with these methods.

The way to handle resistance is to clarify and understand it. Once you clarify each element of resistance so that you completely understand it, you can deal with it. It is much easier to develop persuasive evidence to overcome specific argument than it is to "shoot in the dark." If you know what opinions or ideas conflict with yours, you are better able to develop information to neutralize them.

By asking questions such as how, why, what, where and when, you can clarify resistance. Once you have a thorough understanding of the resistance, you can develop point by point information that will help you neutralize the resistance and persuade others to accept your point of view.

Use Constructive Questioning

Some people hesitate to ask questions because they think it is manipulative or that the answers will be personal. Questions are not manipulative, people sometimes are. Questions are only personal when people make them so. You can easily avoid this problem by always using questions in a constructive way. The following questioning techniques will help you gather information that will support your persuasive efforts. These questions can be classified as qualifying, supposition, justifying, alternative, and fact finding.

Qualifying questions. Qualifying questions are those that are used to bring a statement into perspective in relation to its results. For example, you might ask, "How will this benefit you?" or, "What will we get out of this?" Another qualifying question might be, "What will the long term result of this be?" Any question that places emphasis on the results is a qualifying question and will improve your persuasive efforts.

Supposition questions. The supposition question is very effective in getting another to evaluate his own position. You can get him to look at a broader perspective by asking how his idea or plan would work under various conditions.

You might say, "Suppose we were faced with the social issue?" By explaining how the idea applies to the social issue you introduced, the person explaining his or her idea is forced to think through the social implications and evaluate his or her idea from that perspective. Depending upon the nature of the idea, the supposition could also be related to financial, moral, religious, or political issues. Any of these will cause the other person to evaluate his idea and will help you in your persuasive efforts.

Justification questions. A justifying question is simply one that asks the other to justify his or her statement. When someone makes a general statement such as, "Interest rates will go down next month," you are entitled to some supporting data. So, ask for some justification for the statement. Say, "Can you justify that?" Or, a more polite way might be to ask, "What do you base that on?" Or, "Why do you say that?" Any question that requires the other person to justify his opinion will cause him or her to rethink and reevaluate that opinion.

Alternative questions. Questions that require comparison or contrast are alternative questions. These give the other person choices, and may be used to get him to evaluate his own ideas or to gain acceptance for one of your own. Ask, "Do you like A or B best?" Or, "What do you think of your idea as compared to that of Mr. Jones?" Or, "Would you compare and contrast your idea with those of Newton?"

Fact-finding questions. Fact-finding questions are those that you are already familiar with. Commonly referred to as the six "W's", they are what, who, where, why, when, and which. The answers to these six questions will give you all the information you need to thoroughly understand the opposing viewpoints that you are trying to overcome.

Summarize Your Evidence and Conclusions

Summarize your evidence to make sure that it has been heard and summarize your conclusions to make sure your evidence was understood. This gives your listener an opportunity to clear up any misunderstandings and gives you an opportunity to check to see if you have achieved understanding.

After summarizing, ask if your point is clear. Say, "Have I made that clear?" Or, "Do you have any questions about this?" Finally, you might ask, "Would you like to discuss any areas that you disagree with?" Often there are hidden disagreements, and this question will bring them out. You can only deal with disagreement when it is in the open, so try to bring it out.

It is also a good idea to summarize the points of disagreement made by the other person. This shows that you listened and it also gives you an opportunity to show how you resolved those disagreements. If you follow this process, you will be highly effective in persuading people to accept your ideas and opinions.

ELEMENTS OF OPINION

Opinions evolve from a combination of elements that form a balance between a person's motivations, ethical considerations, and the consensual support of his or her family, friends, or peer group. By recognizing each of these elements, you can find a

congruent relationship between your opinion and an element of
the other person's opinion and stress that congruence in your
persuasive appeal.

Statements of Appeal

A statement of appeal, intended to change an opinion, must
contain convincing evidence. To convince someone to change his
opinion, you must present logical arguments, provide concrete
examples showing how your opinion or plan will work, use
analogies from the experience of the person or group you are
speaking to, and state general propositions or appeals based upon the evidence you have used.

Consensual Support

To persuade someone to accept your point of view, you must
consider the effect this will have upon this person's association
with friends and peer groups. If the opinion clashes with that of
the peer group, the opinion will generally be discarded in favor of
the one held by the group.

To overcome this problem, you must prepare the person
whose opinion you are trying to change to defend the new
concept against group pressure. You do this by pointing out how
the opinion will benefit the group and how it is consistent (in
balance) with some other ideas held by the group. If the idea or
opinion can be presented to the group as a helpful idea rather
than a harmful one, the group will usually accept the new idea.

Overcoming Previous Convictions

If a previously held conviction is complimentary to your
idea, then use it to support your position. If it conflicts with your
idea, then you must find a way to neutralize it. One way to do
this is to show that the conflicting conviction is inconsistent or
out of balance with other elements of the individual's opinion.
For example, perhaps the conviction is not in agreement with
moral principles expressed by this individual. If these inconsis-
tencies are brought to his attention, he or she will be internally
motivated to regain balance and will often accept your idea.

Using Motivational Support for Your Ideas

The final opportunity to win an opinion change is to tie in to the individual's motivational system. Since everyone is motivated and stays in balance by self-image, a set of values, and a good reputation, you can tie your persuasive appeal to any of these elements to gain support for your idea or opinion.

Using self-image to support your idea. A person who holds a self-image as a kind, benevolent person will respond to ideas that stress kindness or benevolence. When dealing with this type of person, talk up the higher values and beneficial aspects of your idea. If you can point out that the person would be proud to be associated with the idea or that the idea will enhance his or her reputation, so much the better.

If, on the other hand, the person you are conversing with holds an image of himself or herself as a hard-nosed, realistic, dogmatic person, then point out the more dogmatic aspects of your idea. Describe it with phrases such as, "It's a dog-eat-dog world." These harsh statements will fit his or her self-image and be readily acceptable.

Using value-systems and life-style to support your idea. Developing an argument to fit the value-systems and life-style of the person or group you are trying to persuade is similar to fitting your argument to the person's self-image. In both situations you find a fit or consistency between your idea and the values of the other person.

If the person you are conversing with is an economist, then your argument should not violate economic principles. If a religious person, then tie in to the religious aspects of your idea and the religious beliefs of the other person.

In all situations, remember to create balance and consistency. Listen, try to understand the opposing point of view, and your persuasive techniques will be fruitful. Your ideas will prevail.

14

Conversational Techniques That Give You the Magic Sound of a Professional

Although you like most people, may not wish to become a professional speaker, you can use some of the techniques used by professional speakers to improve your conversation in social situations. The professional speaker's techniques for turning his experiences into interesting stories will help you hold the interest of people in social situations. You'll be able to improve your voice and speech patterns and become more poised in any situation by applying methods revealed in this chapter.

The use of visual aids are limited to business and professional presentations, but the use of words to form visual impressions will enhance your popularity and ensure your success in social or business meetings. Finally, in this chapter, you'll learn the secrets professional speakers use to talk on any topic without preparation. You'll learn to use these secrets to talk to anyone at any time on any subject in a calm and relaxed way.

HOW TO TURN YOUR EXPERIENCES INTO INTERESTING STORIES

Most human experiences are interesting in and of themselves. Often, however, people relate their stories in a way that does not develop proper interest. By telling your story in the proper sequence, using humor as appropriate, and adding story-building techniques, you can turn any experience into an interesting story.

Interest-Building Techniques

The same techniques that are used in writing fiction can be adapted to telling your experiences. You can outline your experience in a story format to make it as interesting as any work of fiction by *Setting the stage, Describing an initial action, Relating an internal response* through *Goal-seeking behavior,* telling *The consequences of the protagonist's behavior,* and giving *The conclusion.*

Setting the stage. To set the stage, focus the listener's attention on the situation. Reveal information about the protagonist, the physical environment, and the social aspects of the situation. This information draws the listener's attention. The listener will begin to wonder what actions the protagonist will take, what kind of person the protagonist is, and what adventure will unfold.

The physical and social environment add the key ingredients in setting the stage. Within the physical constraints described, the protagonist must take action to reach his or her objective. The more unusual or dangerous the environment, the more interesting the material becomes. The social setting may also create interest in that it provides the complexity the protagonist must deal with. He may be described as being in harmony with the environment or as being in disharmony with the environment. If you describe the protagonist as being in disharmony with the environment, the listener will become interested in how harmony will be achieved. If you describe the protagonist as being in harmony with his environment, then the listener will wonder what action will be introduced that will disrupt the situation. Either approach develops interest.

Describing an initial action. The initial action is the first episode in the story. The initial action is any event or natural occurrence which affects the protagonist. The effect can be directly upon the protagonist, or it can be upon someone or something that is of interest or value to the protagonist. The protagonist will react in some way that sets the theme for the story.

Relating an internal response. Next, after the initial action, reveal the protagonist's internal response. It may be an emotion such as anger, hate, fear, happiness, excitement or gloom. This emotional response establishes the motivation for the protagonist's future actions.

The internal response may also be a cognitive one such as a sudden insight, inspiration, or realization of a condition such as beauty. The cognitive realization then motivates the protagonist to further action. A decision to begin some course of action is made by the protagonist at this time.

Goal-seeking behavior. The plot deepens, the protagonist puts his or her plan of action into operation. An attempt or series of attempts is made by the protagonist to achieve the established goal. The character and motivation of the protagonist determines the type of behavior that he or she utilizes in reaching the established goal.

If the protagonist is a hostile type, the behavior utilized in seeking the goal will be a hostile aggressive behavior. One of the interesting techniques of plot development is a change in the protagonist's personality. This can take any of a number of forms. The most usual is a change from a hostile to a more mellow personality or a change from a submissive personality to a more aggressive one. Events unfolding during the story usually account for these personality changes.

The consequences of the protagonist's behavior. At this point interest has been built to a high level. Your listener wants to know whether or not the behavior of the protagonist was successful in attaining the identified goal. The listener will have developed an idea about the consequences of the described behavior and will have decided upon some outcome. In the listener's mind this expected outcome will be consistent with the described behavior.

You may wish to develop an unexpected ending to add surprise to your story. If you have a surprise ending, however, you must be able to explain it in relation to past events. In other words, you must find a way to make your unexpected conclusion seem reasonable. Authors do this by dropping clues along the way. These clues are seemingly insignificant at the time they are dropped but become very important when explaining the unexpected conclusion.

The conclusion. When concluding your story, you reveal the protagonist's feelings. Your listener will be interested in the emotional reaction, the cognitive awareness or the final action taken by the protagonist as a result either of success or failure. If the protagonist was successful, then he will most likely express a pleasurable emotion. If, on the other hand, he failed to attain the identified goal, there are a number of options available to the protagonist.

Often, at this point, a previously unrevealed aspect of the protagonist's personality is brought into play. Perhaps the protagonist's strength during crisis will be revealed. Or perhaps some weakness or personality problem will be revealed as a cause for the failure. In this final section, your purpose is reinforced, your philosophy vindicated.

How Ted Watt's Story-a-Day Adds Poise and Popularity to His Life

Ted Watt was a reasonably gregarious person who knew many people, attended a number of parties, and was liked by most of those who knew him. Ted talked when someone else led the conversation but had difficulty in leading the conversation himself. He noticed that one of his friends at work always had a story to tell and thought how much more popular he, Ted, would be if he, too, could tell such interesting stories.

Ted talked to his friend and found the secret. The friend revealed that he took the trivial incidents of his life and reconstructed them using the techniques that authors use in writing fiction. By taking a little time each night to apply the writing process to incidents that ocurred during the day, he was prepared with interesting stories for the next day.

Ted got the formula from his friend and began to practice using it each night. He would take such a simple incident as having a flat tire and build it into an interesting story. He set the stage, in the flat tire story, by describing how important it was to be at work on time on this particular day. Then he described the initial action of the tire going flat and the internal response he had. He talked of the tension that built as he worked rapidly to repair the tire.

Ted then recounted his mental attacks on stop signs, traffic lights and the traffic that impeded his progress toward his goal. He then recounted the consequences of his behavior. Ted told of the narrow misses and close scrapes he encountered as he took unnecessary risks to get to work on time. And then the conclusion: Just a block before he reached the office (only three minutes late), he was forced to make an unexpected stop. A policeman stopped Ted and gave him a traffic ticket which caused him to be twenty minutes late. He would have only been five or six minutes late if he had driven safely.

HOW PROFESSIONAL SPEAKERS ADD MAGIC TO THEIR SPEECH

Professional speakers use a variety of techniques to enhance their presentations. Voice, volume, inflection, pitch and tone are fine tuned to capture and hold attention. The professional speaker also uses gestures to emphasize important points. All of these techniques will evolve naturally as a speaker learns to relax. There are two additional techniques, however, that must be learned and practiced. They are the use of humor and the use of visual aids.

Developing Humor

The results of psychological tests have demonstrated that people's favorite jokes are related to special concerns or inner conflict. An incident or remark that overcomes or "puts down" the subject of concern or conflict draws forth empathetic laughter. If you can learn enough about your audience to determine what their concerns are, you can direct your humor at these concerns. To develop humor, you must develop a story that sets up a victim for a put-down in a situation that relates to the inner conflicts or concerns of your audience.

Select a Victim

Selecting a Victim is the most sensitive area in developing humor. If you put down a member of the group you are speaking to, you may antagonize the group and lose the opportunity to make them laugh. This also applies when speaking to one person. Unless you have built a long-term friendship which includes friendly "barbs" at each other, you had better refrain from making your friend the victim.

There are two choices for a victim. One is you, the other a public figure. Public figures, especially those with government positions, are expected to be put down. People will laugh when your humor is critical of a public official because they either sympathize with the hopelessness of the situation or they feel the official is ineffective and deserves the criticism.

The choice of yourself as the victim is sure to get laughs. No one is offended, people respect your willingness to "kid" yourself, and you can joke about any subject you wish as long as you are "kidding" yourself. One way to get people to reevaluate their biases is to make yourself the "butt" of a joke reflecting the bias.

Describe a Familiar Stage

It is best to describe a location that the person or audience you are speaking to is familiar with. If you describe an unfamiliar location, the audience's attention is drawn to the details of the place and away from the story. Many comedians use cities, states or capitals for their setting, because people can easily relate to such a location without distracting their attention from the plot.

The time frame is also important in describing the stage. The more recent the time frame, the more easily it is recalled by the listener. If the listener has to mentally work to fix the location and time frame in his mind, he may miss the point of the story.

Comedians often used today's or yesterday's news stories to develop jokes. By picking an item from the news, they can immediately draw a large audience's attention to a familiar stage. The location is generally familiar and the time frame is recent. You can of course use local professional events or social events that are familiar to your audience. The idea is to make your material relevant to the concerns of your audience.

Explain the Reason

Not only do people want to know why the victim says a particular thing or takes a particular action, they need a plot to follow. When you explain the reason, you begin to establish in the audience's mind a set of expected outcomes for the behavior. It is this set of expectations that make it possible for you to turn your story into a joke or develop humor. By changing the expected outcome to an unexpected one, you develop humor.

End with a Punch Line

A humorous story is nothing without a punch line. The punch line catches the listener off guard by ending the story in an unexpected way. The unexpected can be achieved by: (1) a surprise twist, (2) overstatement or understatement, (3) an absurdity, or (4) a letdown.

1. A Surprise Twist. The surprise twist can take many forms. It can be in words or actions. In either form, the story starts with the building of events or thoughts leading in one direction and then unexpectedly the punch line ends with a twist in the conclusion.

For example, a woman who had been invited to a Fourth of July party insisted that her husband develop the spirit of independence established by our forefathers in 1776. She wanted her husband to buy a colonial style jacket to wear to the party.

Against his better judgment and his wife's quips about his being too tight to spend a few dollars to make the party a success, he accompanied her to a specialty clothing store to look at colonial jackets.

The store clerk quickly noticed the husband's reluctance to buy and joined the wife in a patriotic appeal. The clerk tried unsuccessfully to sell the desired coat at $89.00. The husband used the price as an excuse and said the coat was simply too high. The clerk finally reduced the coat to $79.00.

The husband still refused to buy. He pointed out to the clerk that there were few sales for a coat of this type. "Your price is just too high," concluded the husband. "In exasperation, the clerk relented. "O.K., I'll take $76.00." "That's the spirit," said the husband. "I'll take it."

The twist here is in the husband's attitude. He uses the "Spirit of '76" as a justification for beating the clerk down on the price. This twist is unexpected, yet it is consistent with the details of the husband's concern for money.

2. Overstatement or Understatement. Overstatement (exaggeration) is a very popular type of humor. Think of all the Texas jokes that are based on Texas being bigger and better than anything else in the world. Understatement is just as effective and can be used to generate surprise by switching a Texas joke to the smallest rather than largest.

For example, when I was in grammar school, a big kid moved into town from Texas. He was so big we called him "Big William." I became friends with him and tried to encourage him to be friendly with the other kids. "Big William," however, had always settled his disagreements by fighting. Because he was so large, he usually gave his opponent a thorough beating.

Shortly after I had extracted a promise from "Big William" to be more friendly with the other boys in school, I was told he had just knocked out one of the boys in his gym class. I confronted "Big William" with the admonition that he had promised to be more friendly. "I was more friendly," he replied. "I got it over quick—with one punch!"

An understatement is the statement made by a person to describe a large gain and then use a term to minimize it. For example, a man described the possible gains to be made in a business venture as being four to five hundred percent the first year. He then said his estimate was "conservative, of course."

3. An Absurdity. Humor can also be developed with an absurd ending. The absurd ending must be a surprise. It must be relevant but at the same time ridiculous. Today, people are fed up with inflation. Anything that relates to inflation that can be developed into an absurd situation will get a laugh.

For example, a young man discouraged with the price of food saw a sign in a restaurant, "All You Can Eat for $1.95." He went in and ordered the $1.95 special. After finishing the first order he called the waitress for seconds. Instead of the waitress, a large tough looking waiter came over to the young man's table.

"I'd like seconds; the sign said 'All You Can Eat for $1.95'," stated the young man. "That's right," replied the waiter pointing to the young man's plate, "and that's all you can eat for $1.95."

4. A letdown. The letdown begins with a buildup of a thought that is noble or inspiring and ends with a surprise reversal or letdown. A letdown can occur in many ways. If your audience expects one person to be let down, you can change to someone else.

I have a friend who became so drunk that he wound up in a psycho ward. The next day, he told the attendant that he was not crazy and wanted out.

The attendant took my friend to the doctor in charge who began an examination. The doctor began with a simple comprehension test. He held up his hand and said to my friend "Count my fingers." My friend replied, "No! I'm not dumb enough to fall for that. If I start counting, I'll never get out of here." He looked the doctor in the eye and said, "I don't have to count, you've got five fingers and one thumb." The doctor replied, "Get him out of here, only a drunk would say that."

Historical events can also be used to develop humor. For example, after the Pharoah kicked Moses out and ordered that the name of Moses be removed from all temples and erased from all tablets and never be spoken again, a man met Moses in the market place and asked his name. "I can't remember," replied Moses, "It's been erased."

Using Visual Aids

Professional speakers use visual aids because they know that people learn more through sight than any of the other four senses. It has been estimated that over 80 percent of what we learn is through sight. So, if sight is the most important of the five senses, then visual aids are important in speaking.

Obviously you can't walk around with a suitcase full of charts and graphs or attend a social event with posters tied to your back. You can, however, create your own visual aids with gestures and word pictures. You can use gestures to generate a picture of movement, location, size, speed, and contour. You can use word pictures to relate detail, color, action, feelings, emotions. Anything you can picture in your own mind, you can describe for others.

Visuals are used by professionals to support their spoken word. For example, a speaker said, "The fisherman's line glided through the air accompanied by the sound of the whirring reel, releasing 30 or 40 feet of line to gently splash into the smooth flowing water."

A gesture of a moving arm imitating a graceful cast accompanied the first line. The gesture supported the words describing the line in action. Word pictures were formed with the words "the sound of the whirring reel." In conjunction with the words "releasing 30 or 40 feet of line," the speaker opened a previously tightened fist, spread his fingers apart, moved his open hand forward and downward, and the audience easily completed the picture in their minds. They could see the fisherman's line glide gently through the air. And to accompany the words "to gently splash," the speaker used a soft, inaudible, clapping of the hands, separated into barely perceptible vibrating fingers, then drew his hands back to his sides to imitate the "smooth flowing water."

If you take the time to think through the pictures you wish to describe, you can do so. You can add action, color, distance, size, sound, or any dimension to your speech with gestures and word pictures. Yes, you can add the magic of the professional speaker to your speech.

How Tony Raffaelli Drew Pictures in the Air

Tony Raffaelli used gestures and word pictures in his daily conversation. Many of his peers joked and kidded him about "drawing pictures in the air." A common remark made to Tony was, "You couldn't talk if your hands were tied." But Tony was very effective in telling jokes, relating stories, or giving directions.

On one occasion, Tony told his friends the story of his first interview with the company president. He had just been promoted to supervisor and wanted some policy guidance from the president. In the interview Tony asked the company president, "Will you give me your management philosophy in one sentence?" The president thought for a minute and said, "When you've got them by the throat," (at this point Tony clasped both his hands around his own throat and coughed out the balance of the statement). "When you've got them by the throat (cough!) their hearts and minds will follow."

HOW TO PARTICIPATE IN ANY CONVERSATION WITHOUT PREPARATION

There are two commonly used systems, both currently taught by Toastmasters International, that will help you participate in any conversation without preparation. These methods help beginning speakers prepare speeches, but they are just as effective in impromptu speaking. By mastering the key words in either or both systems, you will be able to speak extemporaneously on any subject at any time. One is the Borden System and the other is the Historical Outline.

The Borden System

Professor Richard C. Borden, who taught speech at New York University, developed the Borden System to reflect the listener's reactions to what is being said. It has four steps which are *Ho-Hum* (boredom), *Why bring that up?* (What's it to me?), *For instance* (Give an example), and *So what* (What should I do?). These steps can be guides for impromptu speaking. By following them, you will be able to participate in any conversation without prior preparation.

How to break the ho-hum barrier. To break the ho-hum barrier, you must do something immediately to catch your listener's attention. This can be done by relating a common human experience, asking a relevant question, or telling an appropriate story. A common human experience is something that everyone has gone through. You might recount about getting your first job or first apartment, getting married, buying something that didn't work, or any other common experience that you can connect with your story. The important point is that the experience be one that everyone can relate to so that you can bridge the experience into your talk.

Asking a relevant question is an excellent attention getter. It breaks the ho-hum barrier because it builds inquisitiveness in the minds of your audience. They wonder why you ask the question, what the answer is, and how it related to your speech. They will pay attention to get the answers. The same effect can be achieved with a strong statement of purpose or challenge that will create interest in what you are going to say to support your statement.

An appropriate story is also a good attention getter that breaks through the ho-hum barrier. Jokes, illustrations, and quotations can be used. The trick is to build the bridge between the joke or quotation to your message or point of view. If it isn't relevant, you must start all over to build interest in your subject matter.

If you can't find a quotation to express the idea you wish to convey, write your own! No one will know the difference. I once gave a speech to a group known to be closed-minded with a reputation for thinking they knew it all. My speech was intended to show that we can all improve if we will open our minds and look and listen for the new information that is all around us.

I couldn't find a quotation that satisfied me, so I wrote my own:

A diminutive spark fell on the darkness of the
universe, and if at that instant my mind were clear and
time frozen, it would take an eternity to absorb all
the knowledge that light revealed!

I pretended the author was unknown, which gave the opening a mystique that also enhanced the message. The audience became quiet and perhaps opened their minds to see what would come next.

Give a reason for speaking on (bringing up) this topic. In this second step, tell your listeners why you are bringing up the topic. Give your audience a reason to listen; show that your topic is important or that it is beneficial or harmful to them in some way.

For example, if a new highway will result in additional commerce, point the benefits of new jobs, lower transportation costs, and lower priced goods and services. By showing how your topic has a direct impact on the lives of your listeners, you generate interest and secure attention to what you say.

Prove your point with evidence. In the third step, you present the evidence. Give facts and figures to prove your point, also illustrations and analogies to get your listener to think about your topic. By relating your topic to other events or ideas that they are aware of, you can get them to think through and generalize from the illustrations to your idea.

You might, for example, encourage people to support a new dam by pointing to the loss to the community from soil erosion or floods. You must gather evidence before speaking to support your point of view. If your conclusions are correct, you should be able to get facts from the library or directly from the Corps of Engineers. Then simply report your findings and state your conclusions as to what effects this will have in the future.

The call to action. The "So What" or fourth step is a call to action. In this step, tell your listener or audience specifically what you want them to do. If a vote is required, ask them each to do their duty by casting their vote. If you're after a letter writing campaign, tell them who to write. Give names and addresses and ask that they write immediately or as soon as they get home. Whatever your purpose is, spell it out clearly, and state the specific action that your audience must take in order to get the job done.

The Historical Outline

The historical outline is the past-present-future approach. This format is especially useful when you are trying to show change that has taken place over time in personal, cultural, or physical development. Start at some time in the past and describe the conditions that existed then. Next describe the changes that have taken place and the results of those changes today. Finally, project those changes into the future; try to show that the continuing changes will result in the condition you describe at some time in the future.

How Ed Blake Won Five Speech Contests Without Preparation

Ed Blake, a member of a local Toastmasters club, had difficulty in making speeches from written material. He didn't sound convincing when he read the material, and notes confused him and caused him to forget what part of the speech he was on. Ed did not have a problem during the impromptu (table topics) session, when speakers had to speak for two minutes without preparation. Ed decided to try all his major speeches without notes, using the following format for speaking without preparation.

1. Make a statement about some past or current event.
2. Explain your personal reaction to the event.
3. Discuss the consequences of the event on individuals, governments, or society.
4. Propose a problem that is related to the event.
5. Pose a question related to the problem.
6. Explain why the problem occurs.
7. Propose ways to deal with the problem.
8. Offer solutions for the problem.
9. Make other suggestions for solutions.
10. Discuss adapting to the new condition.

Ed memorized the ten statements and used them in each speech. He selected some event or topic that he was interested in, researched it, thought about it, went over each of the ten points, and thus prepared himself to speak. Using his new system, he won five of six speech contents that he entered. You can use it too—just memorize the ten step guideline and speak naturally.

15

The Twelve Biggest Mistakes People Make in Conversation and How to Avoid Them

Everyone makes mistakes in conversation as well as in life. There is nothing wrong with mistakes as long as we learn from them. As a matter of fact, making mistakes is one of the ways we learn. We make a mistake, get into a little trouble, or become embarrassed. Then we learn of our mistake and correct it. This is a natural process that helps us grow and mature. A problem arises if we make mistakes and don't learn that we have erred.

You can learn what the twelve biggest mistakes are that people make in conversation. These mistakes occur from habit and people don't usually realize they are making them. This chapter explains how these mistakes occur, the effect they have on other people, and how to avoid them.

THE SIX MOST COMMON CONVERSATIONAL MISTAKES

The mistakes most often made in conversation are those that people make without being aware they are making them. They lose interest and only half listen, or interrupt with another thought. Some people become so interested in the current topic that they interrupt in an attempt to express their own point of view. Others give superficial agreement, make arrogant assertions, or waste time in making excuses. All of these common conversational mistakes interfere with people's popularity and hinder their success.

Listening Superficially

There are many reasons why people listen at a superficial level. Often superficial listening results from a lack of interest in the subject being discussed. If, for example, you have no interest in football, there may be many situations in which football is being discussed; you consequently listen only superficially.

Unfinished thoughts from previous conversations also cause superficial listening. An unfinished thought vies for expression. When you are cut off before you finish expressing a thought or idea, you feel frustrated and are internally motivated to complete the statement. This motivation interferes with your ability to listen because you are preoccupied with the desire to complete your previous thought.

Motivation also distracts when you are tired or bored. You listen superficially then because you are motivated to rest or to find something interesting.

Another cause of superficial listening is unclear explanations. If the person you are listening to is confused or unable to clearly express his or her thoughts, it is difficult to follow, and you turn to superficial listening. Unless you make an extreme effort to listen to people who are unclear, you are likely to listen superficially.

How to Overcome Superficial Listening

There are two basic ways to overcome superficial listening—listen for useful information or ask questions to develop interest. To listen for useful information, you must first realize that most information comes shrouded in extraneous conversation. Always be alert and listen carefully to separate the important from the extraneous. So, simply listen carefully for any information that may apply to something you are interested in. Some of the most creative ideas come from applying in one field the information from another field. If you listen carefully, you may do the same.

By asking questions, you can also develop interest. Ask questions about the topic being discussed that relate to your area of interest, or ask questions for information about the topic being discussed. By learning more about a subject, even one you are not interested in, you will better understand people, expand your area of conversational topics, and will become a more popular person.

Interrupting

It has been said that interrupting is a sign of interest. It does show interest, but not in what the speaker is saying. The person who interrupts is more interested in his or her own thoughts. The interruption is a lack of courtesy. People interrupt for a number of reasons, all of them discourteous. For example, some people become impatient and interrupt. They just can't wait for the speaker to finish his or her comments. Other people become angry and interrupt, and some become so interested and excited they just can't hold back. They just aren't mature enough to restrain themselves and therefore forget to be courteous and let the other person finish his comments.

Interrupting is an attempt to take control of the conversation. Often people make this attempt without realizing what they are doing. By interrupting, you are saying to the other person that what you have to say is more important than what he has to say. In effect, "Shut up. I'm controlling this conversation and I'll do the talking and you'll do the listening."

How to Break the Habit of Interrupting People in Conversation

Obviously, interrupting others will not win you popularity and success but will build resentment and result in a loss of friends. You can break the habit, if you have it, by realizing that interrupting shows a lack of respect and is a hostile action toward others. You can be more effective and popular if you correct the habit.

In addition to being aware of the consequences of interrupting, you should practice controlling your urge to interrupt. When you catch yourself interrupting, stop and apologize. This way you show that the interruption is not intentionally hostile. If you are not sure whether or not the other person is through speaking,

ask before you speak. Simply say, "Are you through?" By following these suggestions, you will slowly overcome the habit of interrupting and become more popular and more successful.

Getting off the Track

Another common conversational mistake is getting off the
track or straying away from the point. Many people have a
problem in structuring their conversation and consequently
stray from the topic of conversation. These people often have a
problem completing one thought without starting another. This
is very irritating to the listener and causes resentment and a lack
of respect.

How to Stay on the Track

To stay on the track and get your point across, practice
these guidelines: (1) Speak in clear and concise terms. (2) Don't
bunch ideas. (3) Use concrete words.

Speak in clear and concise terms. A clear and concise statement won't make the other person accept your point of view, but
at least he or she will be able to understand it. To be clear, you
need only use short, simple, everyday words. Many people will
not know the meaning of "prevaricator," but everyone knows
what a "liar" is. If you feel a need to practice using big or new
words, you should save them for close friends. Otherwise keep
your words short and simple to improve understanding.

To be concise you must keep your message short. One idea
coupled with one descriptive phrase is a good guideline. People
cannot absorb a long sentence complicated with numerous ad-
jectives and adverbs. If three or four descriptive phrases are
needed to complete an explanation, convert them into separate
sentences. Most people can't understand long complicated sentences.

Don't bunch ideas. People can only absorb one idea at a
time. Don't try to save time by rushing through one idea after
another. You should present one idea and then check for understanding before proceeding to the next.

An idea should always be presented in a concise form, not cluttered with a lot of irrelevant material. Supporting material is needed only to clarify the main points.

Use Concrete Words. When the main idea is presented in concrete words, very little explanation or support is needed. So ideas should be presented in concrete words whenever possible. When your idea is presented in abstract words, then you will need to give examples. These examples should be stated in concrete words—specific in number, color, shape, or activity.

You can imagine the difference in images that appear in a person's mind from the word goodness. To one person the word goodness may mean "doesn't kick dogs," to another person it may mean "contributes generously to the church." In order to be certain that the other person visualizes what you mean by goodness, you had better give an example, and the example should be given in concrete words.

Giving Superficial Agreement

People often give superficial agreement rather than confront an issue they disagree with. They feel a confrontation will result in argument or hurt the other person's feelings. So they pretend to agree in order to avoid what they feel would be an unpleasant situation. This superficial agreement cannot be depended upon, and people soon recognize this. Once people become aware that someone is giving superficial agreement, they lose respect for and distrust that person.

How To Correct the Superficial Agreement Mistake

If you have developed a habit of agreeing with people, even when you really aren't convinced of their position, you are leaving an impression that is just the opposite of the one you think you are leaving. People have more respect for a person who expresses his own convictions than they do for someone who agrees superficially in an attempt to be nice.

You can overcome this mistake, by withholding agreement until you are sure you accept the other person's opinion. If you don't agree, ask for further explanation. If you agree with part of what is being said, say that you agree with that part. Finally, you don't have to start an argument to disagree. Simply say, "I don't share that opinion," or "I have a different opinion," or "I feel differently about that." Then very calmly express your opinion. Don't argue or become angry, just express your opinion and you will gain more respect and popularity.

Making Arrogant Assertions

People who make arrogant assertions don't realize they are being arrogant. Usually they feel they really know a lot and they are simply sharing their knowledge with others. Arrogant statements, however, very quickly turn people off. Many arguments are started in response to arrogance. People often attack an idea, not because they reject the idea but because they can't stand the arrogance of the person making the statement.

How To Correct the Arrogant Assertion Habit

Since arrogance is usually not recognized by the arrogant person, we must all assume that at some time, in some situation, we are probably arrogant. The remedy is to always express our statements as opinions, thoughts or feelings. If you always start your sentences with, "I think, In my opinion, I feel," or "As I see it . . .," you will be less likely to come across as arrogant.

Making Excuses

The only time an excuse is appropriate is when you are specifically asked how something happened. Usually, however, people make excuses to cover their mistakes or carelessness. These people satisfy themselves because they think they have convinced the other person that they were not responsible for what happened. This is usually not true. More often, the other person believes that you simply can't handle the situation and additionally are not willing to take responsibility for your own actions.

How To Stop Making Excuses

This is the easiest mistake of all to stop. Simply stop! You can stop making excuses, but this means you must pay more attention to what you are doing and get it right. If you need help or make a mistake, get someone to help you immediately. Don't wait for "excuse time" to correct errors. Correct them on the spot. Don't be afraid to admit that you need help, and you'll never need to make excuses.

HOW TO OVERCOME THE SIX MOST DAMAGING REASONS FOR FAILURE IN CONVERSATION

We can never completely eliminate failure in conversation but we can substantially reduce it. There are times when, in spite of our best efforts, we will forget and fall back into old habits that are damaging in conversation. There are six basic reasons for failure in conversation which we can analyze and overcome. These are: (1) arguing, (2) manipulation, (3) forcing a point of view, (4) making sarcastic remarks, (5) criticizing people in public, and (6) not responding in conversation.

How to Stay Out of Arguments

Arguments usually result from attitude problems. For example, you may become angry and shout, threaten, warn, preach, ridicule, shame, criticize, or strike the other person. All of these actions are the result of attitude problems. Your attitude must be that somehow this behavior will accomplish what you could not accomplish through logical discussion. This is an illogical attitude.

Anger can be controlled. You can learn to raise your tolerance level by practicing being more patient with others. Recognize that the small irritations you encounter are not worth the tension that accompanies anger. By becoming aware of the situations that cause anger, you can ask questions to analyze the value of what is being said rather than argue. Ask for more information, more facts, and more examples. If the other person still seems to be wrong, ask, "How sure of this are you?" If he or she isn't sure, he will begin to backtrack and come closer to your position. Then you may calmly present your opinion.

How to Correct Habits of Manipulation

Manipulators use many tricks but most of them fail. They are selfish and have little concern for other people. The fact that they are willing to manipulate people indicates that they hold a low opinion of others and believe they can outsmart them.

The manipulator makes promises but never intends to keep them. He leads people into building up unreal expectations. He does whatever is necessary to get his own way. He hides facts that might lead the other person to a conclusion different than the one he proposes. He improperly evaluates the facts that he presents, building false impressions leading to unreal expectations.

The manipulator distorts the facts. He makes changes in the facts to the extent he feels he can get away with. If he feels the other person has no knowledge of the event being discussed, he will completely alter the facts to support his own conclusion.

Another trick of the manipulator is to manufacture quotations and ascribe them to some well known and respected person. By using such a person, he hopes to add credence to his position.

The use of falsified reports, facts, figures, and statistics is the normal strategy for the manipulator. He misleads another by falsifying the figures or by making false generalizations from the figures.

False analogies, circular reasoning, psychological and other fallacies are used to manipulate the other person's thoughts. Sometimes these unethical methods work for a short time, but usually they fail. In the long run people become aware of the trickery and misrepresentation.

Those who try to manipulate others are always surprised when they are found out. Since their basic beliefs place other people in a "simpleton" category, they are always surprised when exposed.

If you have developed a habit of manipulating people, you can gain popularity, improve your personality, and win new friends by simply correcting this damaging habit. Recognize the fact that manipulation will not work in the long run. You can fool people for awhile, but very soon they get wise. Be aware, also, that you can be more effective by treating others with respect. Express your opinion, but let them make up their own minds and make their own decisions.

How to Break the Habit of Forcing Your Point of View

The first step in breaking the habit of forcing your point of view on others is to realize that you can't force ideas. A person automatically rejects pressure. When you physically push someone, he rejects you by pushing back. When you push an idea, he rejects the idea.

To break the habit of forcing your ideas, concentrate on methods that have been successful in getting people to accept ideas from others. Concentrate on using questions that lead to your conclusion. This system goes all the way back to Socrates and is still effective. Asking for opposing viewpoints also helps get your idea across because it shows that you are not afraid to evaluate other ideas against your own.

When you offer proof for your conclusion, offer it as evidence to be discussed and evaluated. This permits anyone with reservations to talk them out and get them out of the way. Be willing to explore opposing viewpoints. Evaluate their effectiveness and discuss their weaknesses. This encourages the other person to do the same and results in an open-minded reaction to your ideas.

How to Correct the Habit of Making Sarcastic Remarks

People who make sarcastic remarks do so from habit or from a desire to be humorous. Unfortunately, for the sarcastic jokester, most people do not find sarcasm funny.

If you have been using sarcasm in an attempt to be humorous, you are probably irritating many people even though they laugh. You can overcome this problem by substituting other types of humor. Develop one liners or memorize jokes to tell instead of being sarcastic.

If you have been using sarcasm to generate humor, it will probably be easy for you to switch to other types of humor. You probably already have a sense of humor, so all you have to do is direct it at yourself or at politicians. The information in this book can also help you develop additional humor. Other techniques in this chapter will help you develop pleasing personality traits that will win back any respect you may have lost with sarcasm in the past.

How to Avoid Criticizing People in Public

The way to avoid criticizing people in public is to stop criticizing people, period. Criticism is only effective when it is asked for. People do not accept criticism and do not generally try to correct behavior that has been criticized. This would different if a great number of people criticized the person who is acting in an unpopular way. This does not happen, however, so a single criticism is rejected and the person resents you for the criticism.

There is another way to correct inappropriate behavior and that is to lead that person to the realization that the behavior is inappropriate. One way to do this is through questioning. You can ask the person whose behavior you are trying to correct, how he or she feels about the results of his action. Then ask how he feels the specific (questionable) behavior affects those results. For other questioning techniques, see my book, *How to Use Psychological Leverage to Double the Power of What You Say* (Parker Publishing Company, Inc., 1978).

Rather than criticizing people, simply point out that you are upset, offended, distressed, insulted, or disturbed by the behavior of the offending person. By relating your own feelings, you are not criticizing the other person, you are simply point out that you are being hurt by that person's behavior. From a normal person, an apology will follow.

How to Prepare to Respond in Conversation

Most people, at one time or another, are at a loss for words. They simply can't think of anything to say, or they have no information about the topic being discussed. You can overcome this problem by preparing for conversation in advance.

First, list the topics of conversation that come up for discussion during a two week period. Each day write down the topics that are discussed by each of your peer groups, and at the end of two weeks, group them together in like categories. You'll be surprised how few they are.

Once you have the list, you can prepare for daily conversation. Read newspapers, listen to talk shows, ask questions of other people, and in all cases takes notes. Finally, put your ideas together in a written paragraph, review it each night, and you'll be great in conversation every day. You'll be able to join any conversation with logical comments or questions.

Conclusion

You may not believe in "magic"—neither do I. I do believe, however, in the almost *magic* results that people achieve when they employ the techniques of Conversational Magic. I've seen them used over and over to build success after success. I know they work for others and they can for you. If you'll practice the techniques of Conversational Magic, you'll become a happier, more productive person. You'll gain new friends who, along with your current friends, will admire your magic charm, poise, popularity, and success.

SUGGESTED FURTHER READINGS

Braude, Jacob M. *Braude's Treasury of Wit and Humor.* Englewood Cliffs, N.J.: Prentice Hall, Inc., 1978.

Dickens, Milton. *Speech: Dynamic Communications.* 3rd Ed. New York: Harcourt, Brace, Jovanovich, Inc., 1974

Donaldson, Les. *Behavioral Supervision: Practical Ways to Change Unsatisfactory Behavior and Increase Productivity,* Addison-Wesley, 1980.

Donaldson, Les. *How to Use Psychological Leverage to Double the Power of What You Say.* West Nyack, New York: Parker Publishing Co., Inc., 1978.

Hegarty, Edward J. *How to Talk Your Way to the Top.* West Nyack, New York: Parker Publishing Co., Inc. 1973.

Hegarty, Edward J. *Making What You Say Pay Off.* West Nyack, New York: Parker Publishing Co., Inc. 1968.

Hovaland, C., I. Janis and H. Kelley. *Communication and Persuasion: Psychological Studies of Opinion Change.* New Haven, Conn.: Yale University Press, 1961.

Lewin, Kurt. *Resolving Social Conflicts.* (Edited by Gertrude Weiss Lewin). Forest Grove, OR: Souvenir Press, Internation Scholarly Book Services, Inc., 1978.

Minnick, Wayne C. *The Art of Persuasion.* 2nd ed. Boston: Houghton Mifflin Co., 1968. Copyright © 1963 by Jesse S. Nirenberg, Ph.D.

Rogers, Carl R., Ph.D. *On Becoming a Person.* A Therapist's View of Psychotherapy. Boston: Houghton Mifflin Co. Copyright © 1970 by Carl R. Rogers.

Index

Phrases (*Cont.*)
  to comment on performance, 60
  concrete, 177
  to create enthusiasm, 59
  to create positive impressions, 58-63
  for favorable image, 53
  to praise others, 53
  to reveal expertise, 60-61
  to show respect, 59-60
Plans, 22
Point of view, forcing, 209
Poise, 51-58, 75, 79
  at parties, 133-134
Popularity, 28, 33, 46, 79, 117, 122
  at parties, 131-134
  short cuts to, 127-138
Positive attitude, 89-90
Positive impression, 111
Positive feelings, 44
Praise, 52-53, 68-69, 157, 158
Pressure, 170
Preventing unfounded statements,
    107-108
Pride, 165
Probing, 120-122 (*see also* Mirroring,
    Ventilation)
Problem, focus on the, 179
Psychological barriers, 28-34
Psychological "cooling system," 33-35
    (*see also* Probing Ventilation)
Psychological techniques, 81-92 (*see also*
    Conversational techniques)
  to add interest to conversation, 20-28
Puns, 142-143

Q

Quotations, 143, 198
  rewording, 87
  use of, 86-88
Questions, 21, 41, 98-99, 100, 166, 178, 210
  alternative, 183
  answers to, 53-55
  antagonistic, 112
  background, 66
  constructive, 182-183
  directed, 101
  examples of, 123, 124
  explanatory, 112
  fact-finding, 183
  functional, 83-84
  high receptivity, 123
  hypothetical, 112

Questions (*Cont.*)
  information-gaining, 94-96, 112
  of interest, 85
  justification, 182
  personal, 54-55
  qualifying, 182
  supposition, 182

R

Rapport, conversational, 108-109
Reading, 77
Reassurance, 157
Recognition, 157, 158
Recreation, 77
Refusal to listen, 168-169
Repetition, 177
Research findings, 132
Resentment, 90, 168
Resistance, 181
Respect, 20, 21, 59-60, 92, 99, 102, 110,
    142-144
Response:
  to emotions, 83
  to excitement, 84
Restatement, 108, 179-180
Restaurants, local, 71
Rules, successful conversation, 20-23

S

Sarcasm, 19, 28-30, 43, 84, 100, 117,
    209-210
Secret, 141
Segmented approval, 85
Self-confidence, 52
Self-esteem, 134, 145
Self-image, 157, 159-161, 185
Self-improvement, 76
Shyness, 102-103
  overcoming, 134-137
  at parties, 134
Sideswipe, 30-31
Silence, 20, 21, 42-43, 67-68, 141, 148
Sorrow, 83
Speech:
  concise, 204-205
  non-critical, 145
Sports, 67, 77, 96, 106, 132
Stage, 192
Statements, non-negotiable, 118-119
Story telling, 188-191
  conclusion, 190
  goal-seeking behavior, 189
  setting the stage, 188